Ordnanc

Brecon Beacons and Glamorgan Walks

Pathfinder Guide

Compiled by Brian Conduit

Key to colour coding

The walks are divided into three broad categories, indicated by the following colours:

Short, easy walks

Walks of moderate length, likely to involve some uphill walking

More challenging walks, which may be longer and/or over more rugged terrain, often with some stiff climbs

Acknowledgements

My thanks to the following for their valuable advice and assistance: Roger Stevens and Sarah Williams (Brecon Beacons National Park) and Dennis Watson (Glamorgan Heritage Coast Centre). Also thanks to Phil Phillips of the Vale of Glamorgan Ramblers' Association for checking one of the routes.

While every care has been taken to ensure the accuracy of the route directions, the publishers cannot accept responsibility for errors or omissions, or for changes in details given. It has to be emphasised that the countryside is not static: hedges and fences can be removed, field boundaries can alter, footpaths can be rerouted and changes of ownership can result in the closure or diversion of some concessionary paths. Also paths that are easy and pleasant for walking in fine conditions may become slippery, muddy and difficult in wet weather and stepping stones over rivers and streams may become impassable. If readers know of any changes which have taken place, or have noticed any inaccuracies, Jarrold Publishing would be grateful to hear from them.

Ordnance Survey   ISBN 0-319-00372-8
Jarrold Publishing   0-7117-0671-9

First published 1994 by Ordnance Survey and Jarrold Publishing

Ordnance Survey
Romsey Road
Maybush
Southampton SO9 4DH

Jarrold Publishing
Whitefriars
Norwich NR3 1TR

© Crown copyright 1994

Printed in Great Britain by Jarrold Printing, Norwich. 1/94

Previous page: *Llanthony Priory*

Contents

Introduction to the Brecon Beacons and Glamorgan

A glance at a map reveals two potential areas of confusion that need to be cleared up right from the start: what exactly is meant by the Brecon Beacons and what is the relation between the Black Mountains and the Black Mountain? This possible confusion arises from the fact that within the boundaries of the Brecon Beacons National Park there are four separate mountain ranges. The most easterly is the Black Mountains, the Brecon Beacons themselves constitute only the central range despite giving their name to the whole area, to the west of them lies Fforest Fawr, and the most westerly range of all is the Black Mountain. For the remainder of this introduction 'Brecon Beacons' will be used for the national park as a whole and 'central Beacons' when referring specifically to the main central range.

The national park has fairly clearly defined boundaries. In the east the most easterly ridges of the Black Mountains overlook the undulating country leading to the Wye Valley and the English border and at times coincide with the border. The northern boundary is formed by the hills and moorlands of mid Wales and by the western reaches of the Usk valley, before the River Usk bears south-eastwards to flow between the Black Mountains and the central Beacons. In the west the broad, lush vale of Towy makes an obvious boundary. But probably the most obvious boundary of all is to the south, although it is more of a historic, economic and environmental boundary: that between rural and industrial South Wales, largely marked by the line of the 'Heads of the Valleys' road between Abergavenny and Swansea.

Physically this southern boundary is hardly a boundary at all as the ridges that enclose and separate the series of narrow, parallel, tightly packed industrialised valleys that once fuelled the Industrial Revolution and exported their coal all over the world, are an extension of the Brecon Beacons. These valleys reach down to the gentler, pastoral country of the Vale of Glamorgan, moving from an industrial to a rural landscape again, and beyond that to the Bristol Channel coast.

Despite a basic similarity and uniformity of geology, each of the four ranges that constitute the Brecon Beacons has its own distinctive characteristics. The Black Mountains, the bulk of which lie to the west of the Wye and north of the Usk with a few detached 'outliers' around Abergavenny, comprise a series of long ridges separating narrow, quiet and still remote valleys. In the central Beacons a steep escarpment rises above the Usk valley to a collection of smooth, rounded summits, the highest in the national park and including Pen-y-Fan (2,907 feet (886 m)), the highest point not only in South Wales but in the whole of southern Britain. Fforest Fawr, the 'Great Forest of Brecknock', was once a royal hunting ground, a bare, austere, lonely moorland area that lies between the upper reaches of the Taff to the east and the Tawe to the west. In the far west is the wildest and most remote area of the national park, the Black Mountain, brooded over by the bold and unmistakable profile of the Carmarthen Fans, Bannau Sir Gaer and Fan Brycheiniog.

The underlying unity of the Brecon Beacons as a whole comes from the area's basically simple geological structure. Most of it is underlain by Old Red Sandstone which gives it certain physical and scenic characteristics that distinguish it from the more rugged mountain areas of North Wales. This is an area of smooth, sweeping grassy uplands, wide and open vistas and, apart from the abrupt north-facing escarpment, gradual rather than steep or major gradients. The northern escarpment, caused by massive earth movements which thrust the mountains up and then tilted them to the south, is the most striking feature, stretching right across the region from the English border to the vale of Towy but seen at its most dramatic in the central Beacons and Black Mountain.

Only on the southern rim does the sandstone give way to overlapping bands of carboniferous rocks, limestone and millstone grit. Here can be found all the common features of Carboniferous Limestone scenery: scars, shake holes, gorges, caves, waterfalls and disappearing rivers. Particularly fascinating is the area to the south of Ystradfellte where the limestone meets the millstone grit, resulting in a series of spectacular falls on the rivers Mellte, Hepste, Neath and Pyrddin, the most concentrated area of waterfalls in Wales.

Youngest of the carboniferous rocks are the coal measures further south which gave rise to the mining industry and led to the tremendous industrial and

Craig y Cilau

population growth in the narrow, parallel valleys of the Rhymney, Taff, Dare and Rhondda which extend like a series of fingers southwards from the mountain core. At their southern end these coal-bearing valleys open out into the Vale of Glamorgan, an undulating limestone plateau that ends in a dramatic and largely unbroken line of cliffs on the Glamorgan coast.

The Brecon Beacons and Glamorgan have their fair share of historic monuments. Prehistoric remains include stone circles, hill forts such as Crug Hywel above Crickhowell and Pen-y-crug above Brecon, and standing stones. Of the latter there are two particularly fine examples, Maen Llia and Maen Madoc, both of which have atmospheric locations, rising amidst the lonely and austere moorlands of Fforest Fawr.

Both Roman and Norman conquerors avoided the mountain barrier to South Wales and took easier lowland routes, either to the north via the Usk valley or to the south via the coast and the Vale of Glamorgan. The Romans have left little in the area apart from some well-preserved sections of road, notably Sarn Helen that runs across Fforest Fawr to the north of Ystradfellte and the 'Gap Road' through the central Beacons, although there is some doubt as to the Roman origins of the latter.

On the other hand the Normans have left a chain of castles along both invasion routes to mark their line of conquest: Abergavenny, Crickhowell, Tretower, Bronllys and Brecon in the Usk and its tributary valleys, and Cardiff, Coity, Ogmore and the New Castle at Bridgend in the Vale of Glamorgan. Two castles must be singled out as particularly outstanding. The finest castle in the national park is Carreg Cennen, perched theatrically on a 300-foot- (91 m) high limestone crag in the foothills of the Black Mountain. Even more impressive is the mighty, lake-girt Caerphilly Castle to the north of Cardiff, second only to Windsor in size among British castles. Its massive concentric fortifications and elaborate water defences made it the most strongly defended castle in Britain.

The Normans also established monasteries around the fringes of the area. The most important of these were the Augustinian priory at Llanthony, beautifully situated in the secluded vale of Ewyas deep in the Black Mountains, the fortress-like Ewenny Priory in the Vale of Glamorgan, and the Benedictine priory at Brecon, elevated to cathedral status in 1923 and bestowing an added distinction on the principal town in the national park. Evidence of an older Celtic Christianity can be found in the fascinating little town of Llantwit Major near the Glamorgan coast, an important centre of learning during the Dark Ages.

Until the nineteenth century the region as a whole was a thinly populated farming area. By and large the Brecon Beacons area has remained that way, with just a handful of small villages and a number of pleasant market towns within or around the periphery of the national park: Abergavenny, Hay-on-Wye, Crickhowell, Llandovery and Brecon itself. But the Industrial Revolution produced a virtual population explosion in the mining valleys to the south, as settlements sprang up along the steep valley sides and merged into each other to form a continuous urban development. The demand for high-quality Welsh coal also led to the rapid expansion of Cardiff, which at the turn of the century was the world's greatest coal exporting port, and the vast bulk of the population of Wales became concentrated in this south-east corner of the country. In recent years the wheel has turned full circle. The mines have closed down, the waste tips have been landscaped and planted with trees, the valleys are becoming green again and the coal industry has started to recede into the area's heritage.

Although the Brecon Beacons largely escaped the ravages of the Industrial Revolution, the twentieth century has made two major physical impacts on the area: the planting of conifer forests and the construction of reservoirs to serve the large towns and industrial areas to the south. Initially regarded as alien intrusions in the landscape, they both now contribute to the region's tourist attractions. Nowadays tourism has become a vital part of the local economy – as it also has in Glamorgan where the combination of impressive scenery and industrial heritage has created a uniquely interesting area.

The Brecon Beacons National Park has much to offer the walker. Apart from the obvious scenic attractions and walking challenges associated with any mountain area, there is a long tradition of *de facto* access to much of the open hillside and moorland. A further advantage is that a high proportion of the land, especially in the central Beacons, and including the highest peaks, is common land, owned either by the national park or the National Trust.

A word of caution is needed, however. Because of their generally smooth and rounded appearance and the absence of craggy outlines, the Brecon Beacons may not look as daunting or formidable as the mountains of Snowdonia, the Lake District or the Scottish Highlands. But do not be misled. These are true mountains which possess all the potential hazards of other mountain areas and need to be treated with due caution and respect. They have a high altitude and high rainfall, are subject to sudden mists – these are especially dangerous along the edge of the steep northern escarpment – and large areas of Fforest Fawr and the Black Mountain in the west comprise bare, trackless, featureless moorland. Indeed, the area of the Carmarthen Fans in the Black Mountain is one of the few genuinely wilderness areas remaining in southern Britain and the national park authorities are keen to preserve its unique quality of remoteness. Because of this there are no suggested walks in that area but experienced walkers might like to explore it for themselves, armed with the appropriate Ordnance Survey Outdoor Leisure map.

By including some walks to the south of the mountains, in the valleys, vale and coast of Glamorgan, the variety of scenic and historic attractions is extended. In view of their industrial image walkers might well be pleasantly surprised by the amount of attractive and unspoilt country in the former mining valleys, and the church towers and picturesque thatched villages of the Vale of Glamorgan are reminiscent of Somerset and Devon, on the opposite side of the Bristol Channel.

For first-time visitors the Brecon Beacons Mountain Centre near Libanus,

to the south-west of Brecon, is the ideal starting point. Not only is it full of useful information but in fine weather you can sit outside on the terrace relaxing over a light meal and cup of coffee, admiring one of the most striking views in the whole of Wales, a panorama of the highest peaks in the Beacons, the core of the mountain massif. If that does not whet your appetite for exploring this beautiful, wild, fascinating area, nothing will.

Glossary of Welsh words

aber	estuary, confluence
afon	river
bach, fach	small
bont, pont	bridge
bryn	mound, hill
bwlch	pass
caer	fort
capel	chapel
carn, carnedd	cairn
castell	castle
ceunant	gorge, ravine
coed	wood
craig	crag
crib	narrow ridge
cwm	valley
drws	door, gap (pass)
dyffryn	valley
eglwys, llan	church
fach, bach	small
fawr, mawr	big
ffordd	road
foel, moel	rounded hill
glyn	glen
hen	old
llan, eglwys	church
llyn	lake
maen	stone
mawr, fawr	big
moel, foel	rounded hill
morfa	sea marsh
mynydd	mountain
nant	brook
newydd	new
pair	cauldron
pen	head, top
pont, bont	bridge
pwll	pool
rhaedr	waterfall
sarn	causeway
traeth	beach, shore
twll	hole
ynys	island

The national parks and countryside recreation

Ten national parks were created in England and Wales as a result of an Act of Parliament in 1949, and an eleventh was established under special legislation in 1989. In addition to these, there are numerous specially designated areas of outstanding natural beauty, country and regional parks, sites of special scientific interest and picnic areas scattered throughout England, Wales and Scotland, all of which share the twin aims of preservation of the countryside and public accessibility and enjoyment.

In trying to define a national park, one point to bear in mind is that unlike many overseas ones, Britain's national parks are not owned by the nation. The vast bulk of the land in them is under private ownership. John Dower, whose report in 1945 created their framework, defined a national park as 'an extensive area of beautiful and relatively wild country in which, for the nation's benefit and by appropriate national decision and action, (a) the characteristic landscape beauty is strictly preserved, (b) access and facilities for public open-air enjoyment are amply provided, (c) wildlife and buildings and places of architectural and historic interest are suitably protected, while (d) established farming use is effectively maintained'.

The concept of having designated areas of protected countryside grew out of a number of factors that appeared towards the end of the nineteenth century:

principally greater facilities and opportunities for travel, the development of various conservationist bodies and the establishment of national parks abroad. Apart from a few of the early individual travellers such as Celia Fiennes and Daniel Defoe, who were usually more concerned with commenting on agricultural improvements, the appearance of towns and the extent of antiquities to be found than with the wonders of nature, interest in the countryside as a source of beauty, spiritual refreshment and recreation, and, along with that, an interest in conserving it, did not arise until the Victorian era.

Towards the end of the eighteenth century, improvements in road transport enabled the wealthy to visit regions that had hitherto been largely inaccessible and, by the middle of the nineteenth century, the construction of the railways opened up such possibilities to the middle classes and, later on, to the working classes in even greater numbers. At the same time, the Romantic movement was in full swing and, encouraged by the works of Wordsworth, Coleridge and Shelley, interest and enthusiasm for wild places, including the mountain, moorland and hill regions of northern and western Britain, were now in vogue. Eighteenth-century taste had thought of the Scottish Highlands, the Lake District and Snowdonia as places to avoid, preferring controlled order and symmetry in nature as well as in architecture and town planning. But the upper and middle class Victorian travellers were thrilled and awed by what they saw as the untamed savagery and wilderness of mountain peaks, deep and secluded gorges,

The River Towy near Llandovery

thundering waterfalls, towering cliffs and rocky crags. In addition, there was a growing reaction against the materialism and squalor of Victorian industrialisation and urbanisation and a desire to escape from the formality and artificiality of town life into areas of unspoilt natural beauty.

A result of this was the formation of a number of different societies, all concerned with the 'great outdoors': naturalist groups, rambling clubs and conservationist organisations. One of the earliest of these was the Commons, Open Spaces and Footpaths Preservation Society, originally founded in 1865 to preserve commons and develop public access to the countryside. Particularly influential was the National Trust, set up in 1895 to protect and maintain both places of natural beauty and places of historic interest, and, later on, the Councils for the Preservation of Rural England, Wales and Scotland, three separate bodies that came into being between 1926 and 1928.

The world's first national park was the Yellowstone Park in the United States, designated in 1872. This was followed by others in Canada, South Africa, Germany, Switzerland, New Zealand and elsewhere, but in Britain such places did not come about until after the Second World War. Proposals for the creation of areas of protected countryside were made before the First World War and during the 1920s and 1930s, but nothing was done. The growing demand from people in towns for access to open country and the reluctance of landowners – particularly those who owned large expanses of uncultivated moorland – to grant it led to a number of ugly incidents, in particular the mass trespass in the Peak District in 1932, when fighting took place between ramblers and gamekeepers and some of the trespassers received stiff prison sentences.

It was in the climate exemplified by the Beveridge Report and the subsequent creation of the welfare state, however, that calls for countryside conservation and access came to fruition in parliament. Based on the recommendations of the Dower Report (1945) and the Hobhouse Committee (1947), the National Parks and Countryside Act of 1949 provided for the designation and preservation of areas both of great scenic beauty and of particular wildlife and scientific interest throughout Britain. More specifically it provided for the creation of national parks in England and Wales. Scotland was excluded because, with greater areas of open space and a smaller population,

there were fewer pressures on the Scottish countryside and therefore there was felt to be less need for the creation of such protected areas.

A National Parks Commission was set up, and over the next eight years ten areas were designated as parks: seven in England (Northumberland, Lake District, North York Moors, Yorkshire Dales, Peak District, Exmoor and Dartmoor) and three in Wales (Snowdonia, Brecon Beacons and Pembrokeshire Coast). At the same time the commission was also given the responsibility for designating other smaller areas of high recreational and scenic qualities (areas of outstanding natural beauty), plus the power to propose and develop long-distance footpaths, now called national trails, though it was not until 1965 that the first of these, the Pennine Way, came into existence.

Further changes came with the Countryside Act of 1968 (a similar one for Scotland had been passed in 1967). The National Parks Commission was replaced by the Countryside Commission, which was now to oversee and review virtually all aspects of countryside conservation, access and provision of recreational amenities. The country parks, which were smaller areas of countryside often close to urban areas, came into being. A number of long-distance footpaths were created, followed by an even greater number of unofficial long- or middle-distance paths, devised by individuals, ramblers' groups or local authorities. Provision of car parks and visitor centres, waymarking of public rights of way and the production of leaflets giving suggestions for walking routes all increased, a reflection of both increased leisure and a greater desire for recreational activity, of which walking in particular, now recognised as the most popular leisure pursuit, has had a great explosion of interest.

In 1989 the Norfolk and Suffolk Broads joined the national park family, special legislation covering the area's navigational interests as well as aspects of conservation and public enjoyment.

The authorities who administer the individual national parks have the very difficult task of reconciling the interests of the people who live and earn their living within them with those of the visitors. National parks, and the other designated areas, are not living museums. Developments of various kinds, in housing, transport and rural industries, are needed. There is pressure to exploit the resources of the area, through more intensive farming, or through increased quarrying and forestry, extraction of minerals or the construction of reservoirs.

In the end it all comes down to a question of balance: a balance between conservation and 'sensitive development'. On the one hand there is a responsibility to preserve and enhance the natural beauty of the national parks and to promote their enjoyment by the public, and on the other, the needs and well-being of the people living and working in them have to be borne in mind.

The National Trust

Anyone who likes visiting places of natural beauty and/or historic interest has cause to be grateful to the National Trust. Without it, many such places would probably have vanished by now, either under an avalanche of concrete and bricks and mortar or through reservoir construction or blanket afforestation.

It was in response to the pressures on the countryside posed by the relentless march of Victorian industrialisation that the trust was set up in 1895. Its founders, inspired by the common goals of protecting and conserving Britain's national heritage and widening public access to it, were Sir Robert Hunter, Octavia Hill and Canon Rawnsley: respectively a solicitor, a social reformer and a clergyman. The latter was particularly influential. As a canon of Carlisle Cathedral and vicar of Crosthwaite (near Keswick), he was concerned about threats to the Lake District and had already been active in protecting footpaths and promoting public access to open countryside. After the flooding of Thirlmere in 1879 to create a large reservoir, he and his two colleagues became increasingly convinced that the only effective protection was outright ownership of land.

The purpose of the National Trust is to preserve areas of natural beauty and sites of historic interest by acquisition, holding them in trust for the nation and making them available for public access and enjoyment. Some of its properties have been acquired through purchase, but many have been donated. Nowadays it is not only one of the biggest landowners in the country, but also one of the most active conservation charities, protecting well over half a million acres of land, including over 500 miles of coastline and a large number of historic properties (houses, castles and gardens) in England, Wales and Northern Ireland. (There is a separate National Trust for Scotland, which was set up in 1931.)

Furthermore, once a piece of land has come under National Trust ownership, it is difficult for its status to be altered. As a result of parliamentary legislation in 1907, the trust was given the right to declare its property inalienable, so ensuring that in any dispute it can appeal directly to parliament.

As it works towards its dual aims of conserving areas of attractive countryside and encouraging greater public access (not easy to reconcile in this age of mass tourism), the trust provides an excellent service to walkers by creating new concessionary paths and waymarked trails, by maintaining stiles and footbridges and by combating the ever-increasing problem of footpath erosion.

For details of membership, contact the National Trust at the address on page 78.

The Ramblers' Association

No organisation works more actively to protect and extend the rights and interests of walkers in the countryside than the Ramblers' Association. Its aims (summarised here) are clear: to foster a greater knowledge, love and care of the countryside; to assist in the protection and enhancement of public rights of way and areas of natural beauty; to work for greater public access to the countryside; and to encourage more people to take up rambling as a healthy, recreational activity.

It was founded in 1935 when, following the setting up of a National Council of Ramblers' Federation in 1931, a number of federations earlier formed in London, Manchester, the Midlands and elsewhere came together to create a more effective pressure group, to deal with such contemporary problems as the disappearance and obstruction of footpaths, the prevention of access to open mountain and moorland and increasing hostility from landowners. This was the era of the mass trespasses, when there were sometimes violent confrontations between ramblers and gamekeepers, especially on the moorlands of the Peak District.

Since then the Ramblers' Association has played an influential role in

9

Talgarth nestling below the Black Mountains

Charter, a concise summary of walkers' rights and obligations drawn up by the Countryside Commission.

Basically there are two main kinds of public rights of way: footpaths (for walkers only) and bridleways (for walkers, riders on horseback and pedal cyclists). Footpaths and bridleways are shown by broken green lines on Ordnance Survey Pathfinder and Outdoor Leisure maps and broken red lines on Landranger maps. There is also a third category, called byways or 'roads used as a public path': chiefly broad, walled tracks (green lanes) or farm roads, which walkers, riders and cyclists have to share, usually only occasionally, with motor vehicles. Many of these public paths have been in existence for hundreds of years and some even originated as prehistoric trackways and have been in constant use for well over 2,000 years.

The term 'right of way' means exactly what it says. It gives right of passage over what, in the vast majority of cases, is private land, and you are required to keep to the line of the path and not stray onto the land either side. If you inadvertently wander off the right of way – either because of faulty map-reading or because the route is not clearly indicated on the ground – you are technically trespassing and the wisest course is to ask the nearest available person (farmer or fellow walker) to direct you back to the correct route. There are stories of unpleasant confrontations between walkers and farmers at times, but in general most farmers are helpful and co-operative when responding to a genuine and polite request for assistance in route finding.

Obstructions can sometimes be a problem and probably the most common of these is where a path across a field has been ploughed up. It is legal for a farmer to plough up a path provided that he restores it within two weeks, barring exceptionally bad weather. This does not always happen and here the walker is presented with a dilemma: to follow the line of the path, even if this inevitably means treading on crops, or to use common sense and walk around the edge of the field. The latter course of action often seems the best but, as this means that you would be trespassing, you are, in law, supposed to keep to the exact line of the path, avoiding unnecessary damage to crops. In the case of other obstructions which may block a path (illegal fences and locked gates etc.), common sense again has to be used in order to negotiate them by the easiest method (detour or removal). If you have any problems

preserving and developing the national footpath network, supporting the creation of national parks and encouraging the designation and waymarking of long-distance footpaths.

Our freedom to walk in the countryside is precarious, and requires constant vigilance. As well as the perennial problems of footpaths being illegally obstructed, disappearing through lack of use or extinguished by housing or road construction, new dangers can spring up at any time.

It is to meet such problems and dangers that the Ramblers' Association exists and represents the interests of all walkers. The address to write to for information on the Ramblers' Association and how to become a member is given on page 78.

Walkers and the law

The average walker in a national park or other popular walking area, armed with the appropriate Ordnance Survey map, reinforced perhaps by a guidebook giving detailed walking instructions, is unlikely to run into legal difficulties, but it is useful to know something about the law relating to public rights of way. The right to walk over certain parts of the countryside has developed over a long period of time, and how such rights came into being and how far they are protected by the law is a complex subject, fascinating in its own right, but too lengthy to be discussed here. The following comments are intended simply to be a helpful guide, backed up by the Countryside Access

negotiating rights of way, you should report the matter to the rights of way department of the relevant county, borough or metropolitan district council. They will then take action with the landowner concerned.

Apart from rights of way enshrined by law, there are a number of other paths available to walkers. Permissive or concessionary paths have been created where a landowner has given permission for the public to use a particular route across his land. The main problem with these is that, as they have been granted as a concession, there is no legal right to use them and therefore they can be extinguished at any time. In practice, many of these concessionary routes have been established on land owned either by large public bodies such as the Forestry Commission, or by a private one, such as the National Trust, and as these mainly encourage walkers to use their paths, they are unlikely to be closed unless a change of ownership occurs.

Walkers also have free access to country parks (except where requested to keep away from certain areas for ecological reasons, e.g. wildlife protection, woodland regeneration, safeguarding of rare plants etc.), canal towpaths and most beaches. By custom, though not by right, you are generally free to walk across the open and uncultivated higher land of mountain, moorland and fell, but this varies from area to area and from one season to another – grouse moors, for example, will be out of bounds during the breeding and shooting seasons and some open areas are used as Ministry of Defence firing ranges, for which reason access will be restricted. In some areas the situation has been clarified as a result of 'access agreements' between the landowners and either the county council or the national park authority, which clearly define when and where you can walk over such open country.

Countryside Access Charter

Your rights of way are:
- public footpaths – on foot only. Sometimes waymarked in yellow
- bridleways – on foot, horseback and pedal cycle. Sometimes waymarked in blue
- byways (usually old roads), most

'roads used as public paths' and, of course, public roads – all traffic has the right of way

Use maps, signs and waymarks to check rights of way. Ordnance Survey Pathfinder and Landranger maps show most public rights of way

On rights of way you can:
- take a pram, pushchair or wheelchair if practicable
- take a dog (on a lead or under close control)
- take a short route round an illegal obstruction or remove it sufficiently to get past

You have a right to go for recreation to:
- public parks and open spaces – on foot
- most commons near older towns and cities – on foot and sometimes on horseback
- private land where the owner has a formal agreement with the local authority

In addition you can use the following by local or established custom or consent, but ask for advice if you are unsure:
- many areas of open country, such as moorland, fell and coastal areas, especially those in the care of the National Trust, and some commons
- some woods and forests, especially those owned by the Forestry Commission
- country parks and picnic sites
- most beaches
- canal towpaths
- some private paths and tracks

Consent sometimes extends to horse-riding and cycling

For your information:
- county councils and London boroughs maintain and record rights of way, and register commons
- obstructions, dangerous animals, harassment and misleading signs on rights of way are illegal and you should report them to the county council
- paths across fields can be ploughed, but must normally be reinstated within two weeks
- landowners can require you to leave land to which you have no right of access
- motor vehicles are normally permitted only on roads, byways and some 'roads used as public paths'

Key Map

CONVENTIONAL SIGNS 1 : 25 000 or 2½ INCHES to 1 MILE

ROADS AND PATHS
Not necessarily rights of way

M1 or A6(M)	M1 or A6(M)	Motorway
A 31(T)	A 31(T)	Trunk or Main road
B 3074	B 3074	Secondary road
A 35	A 35	Dual carriageway
		Road generally more than 4m wide
		Road generally less than 4m wide
		Other road, drive or track

Unfenced roads and tracks are shown by pecked lines

.... Path

RAILWAYS

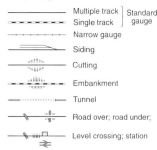

	Multiple track	Standard gauge
	Single track	
	Narrow gauge	
	Siding	
	Cutting	
	Embankment	
	Tunnel	
	Road over; road under;	
	Level crossing; station	

PUBLIC RIGHTS OF WAY   Public rights of way may not be evident on the ground

----------- } Public paths { Footpath
— — — —   { Bridleway

+ + + + + Byway open to all traffic
▲ ▼ ▲ ▼ ▲ Road used as a public path

DANGER AREA
Firing and test ranges in the area
Danger!
Observe warning notices

The indication of a towpath in this book does not necessarily imply a public right of way
The representation of any other road, track or path is no evidence of the existence of a right of way
Public rights of way are not shown on Ordnance Survey maps of Scotland

BOUNDARIES

— · — · — · — County (England and Wales)
— — — — District
–◦––◦––◦––◦– London Borough
. . . . Civil Parish (England)* Community (Wales)
– – – – – – Constituency (County, Borough, Burgh or European Assembly)

Coincident boundaries are shown by
the first appropriate symbol

*For Ordnance Survey purposes
CountyBoundary is deemed to be
the limit of the parish structure
whether or not a parish area
adjoins

SYMBOLS

▪ ▮	Place	with tower
●	of	with spire, minaret or dome
+	worship	without such additions

▢ ▭	Building; important building
▨ ▲	Glasshouse; youth hostel
⬗	Bus or coach station
Ⅱ Λ	Lighthouse; beacon
△ ▲	Triangulation pillar
. T; A; R	Telephone: public; AA; RAC
▦▦▦▦	Sloping masonry
---□----·---- pylon pole	Electricity transmission line
◦ W, Spr	Well, Spring
✛	Site of antiquity
⚔ 1066	Site of battle (with date)

⬬	Gravel pit
⬭	Other pit or quarry
⬮	Sand pit
⬯	Refuse or slag heap
⬮	Loose rock
⬯	Outcrop
⌐⌐⌐	Cliff
⬮	Boulders
⬮	Scree

▭	Water	▭	Mud
▭	Sand; sand & shingle
▬	National Park or Forest Park Boundary
NT	National Trust always open
NT	National Trust limited access, observe local signs
FC	Forestry Commission

VEGETATION   Limits of vegetation are defined by positioning of the symbols but may be delineated also by pecks or dots

⁂	Coniferous trees	◦ ◦ ◦	Orchard	Bracken, rough grassland
◦	Non-coniferous trees		Scrub	In some areas bracken and rough grassland are shown separately
	Coppice		Marsh, reeds, saltings.	Heath

Shown collectively as rough grassland on some sheets

In some areas reeds and saltings are shown separately

HEIGHTS AND ROCK FEATURES

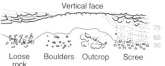

50 ·
285 ·
Determined by { ground survey / air survey }

Surface heights are to the nearest metre above mean sea level. Heights shown close to a triangulation pillar refer to the ground level height at the pillar and not necessarily at the summit

Vertical face

Loose rock   Boulders   Outcrop   Scree

75
60
50

Contours are at 5 metres vertical interval

TOURIST INFORMATION

 Abbey, Cathedral, Priory

 Garden

Other tourist feature

 Aquarium

Golf course or links

Picnic site

Camp site

 Historic house

Preserved railway

 Caravan site

 Information centre

Racecourse

Castle

 Motor racing

Skiing

Cave

 Museum

Viewpoint

Country park

 Nature or forest trail

Wildlife park

 Craft centre

 Nature reserve

 Zoo

Parking

𝕮𝖗𝖔𝖘𝖘
SAILING   Selected places of interest

PC   Public Convenience (in rural areas)

T   Public Telephone

𝔐   Ancient Monuments and Historic Buildings in the care of the Secretary of State for the Environment which are open to the public

Mountain rescue post

National trail or Recreational Path Long Distance Route (Scotland only)

NATIONAL PARK ACCESS LAND   Boundary of National Park access land Private land for which the National Park Planning Board have negotiated public access

Pennine Way   Named path

Access Point

WALKS

 1   Start point of walk

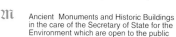 Featured walk

 Route of walk

 Alternative route

ABBREVIATIONS   1 : 25 000 or 2½ INCHES to 1 MILE also 1 : 10 000/1 : 10 560 or 6 INCHES to 1 MILE

BP,BS	Boundary Post or Stone	Mon	Monument	Spr	Spring
CH	Club House	P	Post Office	T	Telephone, public
FV	Ferry Foot or Vehicle	Pol Sta	Police station	A,R	Telephone, AA or RAC
FB	Foot Bridge	PC	Public Convenience	TH	Town Hall
HO	House	PH	Public House	Twr	Tower
MP,MS	Mile Post or stone	Sch	School	W	Well
				Wd Pp	Wind Pump

Abbreviations applicable only to 1 : 10 000/1 : 10 560 or 6 INCHES to 1 MILE

Ch	Church	P	Pole or Post	TCB	Telephone Call Box
F Sta	Fire Station	PW	Place of Worship	TCP	Telephone Call Post
Fn	Fountain	S	Stone	Y	Youth Hostel
GP	Guide Post				

FOLLOW THE COUNTRY CODE

Enjoy the countryside and respect its life and work

Guard against all risk of fire

Fasten all gates

Keep your dogs under close control

Keep to public paths across farmland

Leave livestock, crops and machinery alone

Use gates and stiles to cross fences, hedges and walls

Take your litter home

Help to keep all water clean

Protect wildlife, plants and trees

Take special care on country roads

Make no unnecessary noise

Reproduced by permission of the Countryside Commission

1 Llangorse Lake

Start:	Llangorse Lake
Distance:	3½ miles (5.5 km)
Approximate time:	2 hours
Parking:	Car park at Llangorse Lake
Refreshments:	Pub and café next to car park
Ordnance Survey maps:	Landranger 161 (Abergavenny & The Black Mountains), Outdoor Leisure 11 (Brecon Beacons – Central area) and 13 (Brecon Beacons – Eastern area)

General description *Llangorse Lake, or Llyn Syfaddan, is the largest natural lake in South Wales and is noted for its rich flora and fauna, especially bird life. For much of this flat, easy, relaxing walk around its shores the lake is hidden but from time to time lovely views open up across the water to Mynydd Llangorse. After wet weather the low-lying and badly drained meadows bordering the lake are likely to be waterlogged.*

From the car park walk straight across the field beside it, looking out for a waymarked footbridge over the Afon Llynfi. The whole of this walk is well waymarked and easy to follow. Cross the bridge (**A**), turn half-left and head across a meadow to a stile at the far end. Continue across the middle of a series of meadows, climbing a succession of waymarked stiles and curving gradually to the left all the while. Llangorse Lake is to the left and there are fine views of Mynydd Llangorse and Allt yr Esgair.

On reaching a waymarked post where paths meet (**B**), bear slightly left across the field to a stile beside a metal gate at the corner of a wood. Climb the stile and continue along the right-hand edge of the

Looking across Llangorse Lake

wood, curving left to follow a series of waymarked posts. Cross a footbridge to briefly enter the wood, climb a stile and continue once more along its right-hand edge to another stile. Climb that and head across a meadow in the direction of Llangasty-Talyllyn church, with lovely views opening up across the lake.

Climb a stile just to the left of the church (**C**) and turn right along a track which bears right to continue as a tarmac lane through the hamlet. The church, school and manor house at Llangasty-Talyllyn were all built in the middle of the nineteenth century for Robert Raikes, the founder of the Sunday School movement, to form a religious community. Follow the lane for ½ mile (0.75 km), heading gently uphill to a T-Junction (**D**). Turn right, in the Pennorth direction, and continue for another ¼ mile (0.5 km) as far as a public footpath sign to Ty-Mawr (**E**). Here turn right, climb a stile and walk down a tarmac track towards a farm. Just in front of the farm buildings turn left over a stile, walk along the right-hand edge of a field, by a hedge on the right, and turn right over the next stile.

Head gently downhill along the left-hand edge of a field, by a hedge on the left, climb a stile in the field corner, cross an enclosed path and climb another stile immediately ahead. Bear left to continue along the left-hand edge of a meadow down to a waymarked post (**B**) and a stile just beyond. At the post pick up the outward route and retrace your steps to the start. □

2 Afon Llynfi and Bronllys Castle

Start:	Talgarth
Distance:	4 miles (6.5 km). Shorter version 3 miles (4.75 km)
Approximate time:	2 hours (1½ hours for shorter version)
Parking:	Talgarth
Refreshments:	Pubs and café at Talgarth
Ordnance Survey maps:	Landranger 161 (Abergavenny & The Black Mountains), Outdoor Leisure 13 (Brecon Beacons – Eastern area)

General description *This walk below the northern foothills of the Black Mountains starts unpromisingly with a 1-mile (1.5 km) road walk but develops into a most attractive ramble across fields and meadows bordering the little River Llynfi. The round tower of Bronllys Castle is in sight for much of the way and in the latter stages of the walk there are fine views of Talgarth backed by the long ridge of Waun Fach, the highest point in the Black Mountains. The shorter version of the walk returns directly along the road from Bronllys Castle to Talgarth.*

The walk starts in the centre of Talgarth by the bridge over the River Ennig, in front of the town hall. Head northwards along Hay Road, passing in front of the Tower Hotel, and after ½ mile (0.75 km) bear right (**A**) along the main A4078 road for another ½ mile (0.75 km) – there are wide verges.

Take the first turning on the left (**B**) through a metal gate and follow a winding track to the buildings of Great Porthamel Farm which include a fifteenth-century battlemented tower. Bear left and then right to pass through the farmyard and continue along the track, keeping to the left of the farmhouse. Go through a metal gate and along a hedge-lined track which joins a disused railway track to the left of a bridge. Turn left along the railway track, go through a metal gate, almost immediately turn right through another one, and keep along the right-hand edge of a meadow, by a hedge and wire fence on the right. Later bear left away from the fence to follow a path across the meadow down to the River Llynfi.

Turn left along the riverbank, almost immediately climb a stile, turn right over a footbridge, turn left to climb another stile and bear slightly right uphill along the right-hand edge of a field, by a hedge on the right. At a stile in the hedge turn left and head across the middle of the field – there is no visible path – descending gently to a stile by trees in the bottom left-hand corner. Climb the stile and continue along the left-hand edge of the next field above the wooded riverbank.

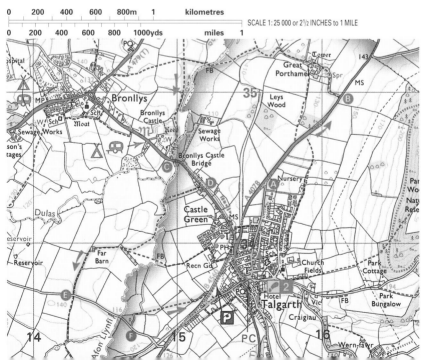

A few yards after passing a yellow waymark on a telegraph pole the path forks; here take the left-hand path which heads down to a stile. Climb it and keep at first by a wire fence on the left and later between wire fences to climb another stile. Walk along the bottom edge of a sloping field to rejoin the river, climb a stile and keep ahead, later descending some steps. Continue along a wooded path by the river to pass below Bronllys Castle, climbing another stile onto a road (**C**). The remains of the castle, little more than a thirteenth-century circular tower, can be visited by turning right, but the route continues by turning left over the bridge across the Llynfi and walking along the road – there is a footpath – beside the River Ennig, a tributary of the Llynfi.

If doing the shorter walk keep ahead along the road back to Talgarth.

At a public footpath sign just after passing the Talgarth sign, turn right along a track (**D**), pass in front of a house, go through a metal gate and walk through a farmyard. Go through another metal gate at the end of it and continue along the left-hand edge of a field, by a wire fence and hedge on the left.

At the end of the field bear slightly right to cross a footbridge over the Llynfi again, turn left alongside the river, climb one stile and continue to another. Climb that and turn half-right to follow the direction of a yellow waymark diagonally and gently uphill across a field, making for the right-hand edge of a line of conifers on the far side. Here go through the right-hand one of two metal gates, bear left, walk along the edge of a field, climb a stile and continue to Far Barn.

At the end of the barn turn left through a large, heavy gate, keep ahead to go through another one, pass between barns and continue along a well-defined, enclosed track, eventually going through a metal gate on to a lane (**E**). Turn left to follow the lane downhill, cross the Llynfi for the last time and about 50 yards (46 m) past the bridge turn left (**F**) along a hedge-lined track bordering a plantation on the left. At the corner of the plantation turn right through a metal gate and climb a stile a few yards ahead. Cross a footbridge over a ditch and continue across a field, making for a metal gate at the far end.

Go through the gate, walk across the next field, go through another metal gate and continue along a hedge-lined track, passing through a metal gate onto a road. Turn right and after a few yards turn left and left again along High Street to return to Talgarth town centre. ☐

3 New Inn and Capel-Gwynfe

Start:	New Inn pub, on A4069 5 miles (8 km) south of Llangadog
Distance:	2½ miles (4 km)
Approximate time:	1½ hours
Parking:	Layby on bend just to west of New Inn
Refreshments:	New Inn
Ordnance Survey maps:	Landranger 160 (Brecon Beacons), Outdoor Leisure 12 (Brecon Beacons – Western area)

General description *This is an easy walk because of the distance and lack of any strenuous uphill sections, but as it is in a relatively unknown and unused part of the national park be prepared for some overgrown, uneven and muddy paths in places. The compensations are solitude and some superb views over the austere slopes of the Black Mountain, especially from the higher parts of the walk near Capel-Gwynfe.*

Start by walking northwards from the bend on the A4069 away from the New Inn pub and take the first turn on the left, just in front of a cottage. Head downhill to cross the River Clydach, start to head up and just beyond a chapel turn left (**A**), at a public footpath sign, onto an uphill track. Follow this track first around a sharp right-hand bend in front of a farm, then around a left-hand bend and continue along a path, between a barn on the left and a hedge on the right, up to a metal gate.

Go through the gate and at a fork immediately ahead bear left uphill, passing by a now redundant kissing-gate, along the right-hand edge of a field, by trees and a hedge-bank on the right. At the top end of the field turn right between trees for a few yards and then turn left over a stile to continue uphill along the left-hand edge of a field towards a house. Pass to the left of the house and go through a metal kissing-gate onto a road (**B**).

Turn left to pass through the hamlet of Capel-Gwynfe. From the road there are fine views both sides: to the right over an attractive patchwork of rolling wooded hills, fields and hedgerows, and to the left across the Clydach valley to the bare, austere slopes of the Black Mountain.

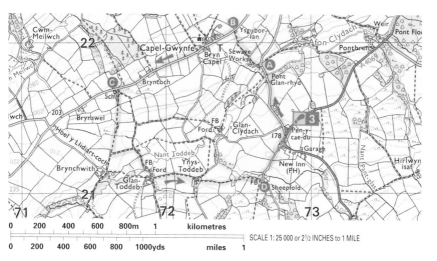

```
0   200   400   600   800m   1        kilometres
|___|___|___|___|___|___|
0   200   400   600   800   1000yds   miles           1
                                      SCALE 1:25 000 or 2½ INCHES to 1 MILE
```

After ½ mile (0.75 km) turn left (**C**) along a hedge-lined track, passing by the left-hand side of a former school building. After the track bears right through a metal gate keep ahead along a path, by a wall and later a hedge on the right, to a metal gate.

Go through the gate and head downhill across a field – there is no visible path – bearing slightly right to pass through a gap in a hedge-bank. Continue in the same direction along a winding, sunken, enclosed path, which is likely to be muddy, heading down to first cross a narrow stream and then climb a stile a few yards ahead. Bear slightly right to follow a path across the next field, go through a metal gate and turn left onto a stony track along the top edge of a field. Follow it as it curves right over a cattle grid to continue as a hedge-lined track.

Cross a stream, keep ahead up to a farmyard and turn left through the far one of two almost adjacent metal gates – the one beside a barn. Go through another metal gate at the end of the barn, continue along the left-hand edge of a field, by a hedge on the left, go through a metal kissing-gate and keep along the left-hand edge of the next field, towards a farm. Go through a metal gate into the farmyard, go through another one and then bear right off the track to pass through the left-hand one of two metal gates in front. Continue along the right-hand edge of a field, by a hedge and wire fence on the right, and descend slightly to cross a footbridge over a stream.

Bear slightly left uphill along the right-hand edge of bracken and then head downhill to keep alongside the stream on the left. At this point there is no visible path and the terrain is rather difficult and uneven. Keeping by the stream all the while, go through a metal gate, almost immediately turn left over a footbridge (**D**) and follow the rough tarmac track ahead uphill for ¼ mile (0.5 km) to return to the start.   □

The Black Mountain from near Capel-Gwynfe

4 The Monmouthshire and Brecon Canal

Start:	Abergavenny
Distance:	5½ miles (8.75 km)
Approximate time:	2½ hours
Parking:	Off Castle Street, Abergavenny
Refreshments:	Pubs and cafés at Abergavenny
Ordnance Survey maps:	Landranger 161 (Abergavenny & The Black Mountains), Outdoor Leisure 13 (Brecon Beacons – Eastern area)

General description *As most of this walk is either across riverside meadows, along a canal towpath or along the track of a disused railway, it is bound to be easy and relaxing. The sections along the banks of the River Usk and the towpath of the Monmouthshire and Brecon Canal are especially attractive and there are some fine views over the Usk valley to the Sugar Loaf and Ysgyryd Fawr. In addition both the canal and the disused railway are of interest to those keen on industrial history.*

Encircled by the outlying hills of the Black Mountains and situated where the River Usk creates a gap in the mountains, Abergavenny guards one of the principal routeways into the heart of South Wales, a position appreciated by the Norman conquerors who built the castle. In the Middle Ages Abergavenny Castle was one of the main border strongholds, the scene of a massacre of Welsh chiefs in 1175, but nowadays little remains and the 'keep' is a nineteenth-century imitation, built as a hunting-lodge and now a museum. More impressive is the large medieval church, originally the chapel of a Benedictine priory, with some fine tombs and choir stalls. Abergavenny lies on the eastern edge of the national park and makes an excellent walking centre.

The walk begins at the entrance to the castle grounds. Facing the entrance turn right and head down the lane beside the castle walls. After about 100 yards (91 m) the lane ends and ahead there are two paths; take the right-hand, lower, one which descends by a wall on the right, and at the bottom turn right onto a paved path. Pass through a metal barrier and continue across a meadow to reach the

bank of the River Usk. In front is a grand view of Blorenge.

Turn right onto another paved path that follows the river along to Usk Bridge (**A**), turn left over the bridge and immediately turn right, at a footpath sign to the cemetery, along a lane. The lane passes to the right of the cemetery and heads gently uphill. At a public footpath sign by a junction of paths and tracks turn left (**B**), in the Llanfoist direction, along a tarmac track – part of the Usk Valley Walk – that heads downhill to pass under a road bridge. Continue along the pleasant hedge- and tree-lined track into Llanfoist (**C**).

Cross a road and continue along the track ahead, which is signposted 'Blorenge and Usk Valley Walk', passing to the right of Llanfoist church and heading steadily uphill between trees. At a fork bear right to an aqueduct but just before reaching it turn right up steps to join the canal towpath. Turn right to follow the towpath for 1½ miles (2.5 km) by the tree-fringed, tranquil waters of the canal, high above the Usk valley with fine views to the right over Abergavenny and the Sugar Loaf, and below the steep, thickly wooded lower slopes of Blorenge on the left. The canal was built between 1797 and 1812 to provide a link between Brecon and the Bristol Channel and carried coal, iron, lime and agricultural produce. After the inevitable decline and fall into disuse, it was restored and reopened in 1970 as a recreational waterway.

At the first bridge turn left over the canal and turn right to walk along the

A peaceful canal scene at Llanfoist

other bank, passing under a second bridge and continuing past a marina by Govilon Boat Club. At a third bridge (**E**) climb steps to leave the canal and turn right along the track of a disused railway, part of a line built in the 1860s to link the coal mines around Merthyr Tydfil, Tredegar and Ebbw Vale to the Monmouthshire and Brecon Canal. Follow the track for just under 1½ miles (2.5 km); it is lined most of the way with attractive willows and silver birches and there are more fine views of Blorenge and the Usk valley. On reaching a T-junction of tracks, pass through a wooden barrier and turn left (**C**) to retrace part of the outward route to the Usk Bridge on the edge of Abergavenny.

Cross the bridge and for the final section you can either continue along the outward route by taking the paved path beside the river, or alternatively head diagonally across the meadows, along a faint but discernible path from which there is a fine view of the castle ruins backed by the distinctive profile of Ysgyryd Fawr. Go through a kissing-gate in the far corner of the meadows and continue to the car parks adjoining Castle Street to return to the start. ☐

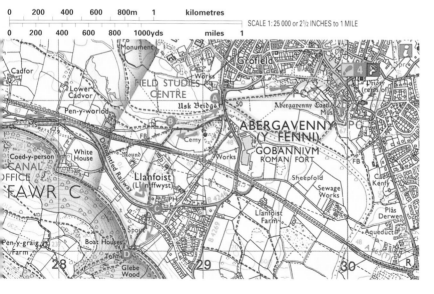

5 Carreg Cennen Castle

Start:	Carreg Cennen Castle
Distance:	4 miles (6.5 km)
Approximate time:	2 hours
Parking:	Car park at Carreg Cennen Castle
Refreshments:	Farm café next to car park
Ordnance Survey maps:	Landranger 159 (Swansea, Gower & surrounding area), Outdoor Leisure 12 (Brecon Beacons – Western area)

General description *The major attraction of this popular and well-waymarked walk in the western foothills of the Black Mountain is the ever-changing views of Carreg Cennen Castle, perched on its precipitous rock, from many different angles. The finale is superb – a steady ascent through beautiful sloping woodland to reach the castle entrance.*

One of the most dramatically sited castles in Britain, Carreg Cennen occupies a 300-foot- (91 m) high exposed vertical limestone outcrop above the Cennen valley. It is everyone's idea of what a ruined castle should be like; it is even complete with an underground passage,

hewn from the rock, which leads down into a cave. Originally a Welsh fortress, stronghold of the Lords Rhys, it was taken by the English and rebuilt and strengthened in the late thirteenth and early fourteenth centuries. Most of its extensive remains belong to that period. Despite its apparent impregnability, it was besieged and captured on a number of occasions and passed through several hands until being largely demolished to prevent its use by brigands after the Wars of the Roses.

At the far end of the car park go through a gate into the farmyard of Castle Farm. Do not continue ahead between the farm buildings towards the castle, but turn right and go through another gate adjacent to a barn. Head downhill across a field, making for a stile and footpath sign in the bottom left-hand corner – like most of the signs on this walk it has a castle symbol on it. Climb the stile and turn left along a narrow lane.

Ignore the first stile on the right and follow the lane downhill, curving left to reach a second stile just before a cottage, at a public footpath sign to Llwyn-bedw (**A**). Turn right over the stile, head downhill across a field, bearing slightly right to climb a stile in the field corner, and continue along a steep downhill path to climb another stile at the bottom. Continue across the next field, cross a footbridge over the River Cennen and bear slightly left to head uphill to a stile. Climb it and continue steeply uphill, keeping parallel with a wire fence and line of trees on the left, towards a farm. In

The dramatic ruins of Carreg Cennen Castle

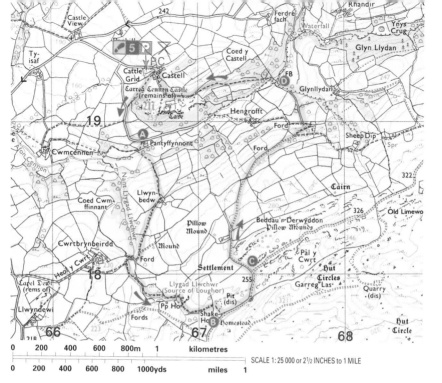

front of the buildings turn right to walk along a track, initially across sloping fields and later continuing through an attractive area of scattered trees. After fording a stream the track bends to the right and then curves left to reach a footpath sign a few yards ahead.

Turn left here over a stile and walk along a track, by a hedge-bank on the right, bearing slightly left to cross a footbridge over a narrow stream and continuing to a stile. Climb it and bear slightly right along an enclosed track; this later emerges briefly into a more open area before continuing as a tree-lined route by the infant River Loughor on the right, a most attractive part of the walk. Climb a stile and if you want to see the source of the Loughor which issues from a cave here, another stile immediately to the right gives access to it.

Continue along the track, which curves slightly left and winds gently uphill, by a wire fence on the right. It then turns left to continue initially by a hedge-bank on the right, and later veers left away from it to a stile. Climb the stile, bear right to pass between two hollows and head across to climb a stile onto a lane (B).

Turn left, climb a stile beside a cattle-grid and continue along the lane as far as a right-hand bend (C). Here keep ahead along a track, by a wire fence and hedge-bank on the right. To the right are the Pillow Mounds, long grassy mounds that look like burial chambers but which were artificial rabbit warrens made by local people in the nineteenth century to ensure a regular supply of fresh meat. The track curves left to a stile; climb it, keep ahead to climb another and continue straight across the middle of a field, bearing slightly left to a gate.

Go through, continue along the left-hand edge of a field, by a wire fence on the left, climb a stile in the field corner by gorse bushes and keep ahead along a sunken grassy track above the steep Cennen valley, now heading downhill. At a fork take the left-hand, lower track which bends sharply left at a footpath sign and continues down to a crossroads of tracks and paths. Climb the stile straight ahead, descend steps and continue downhill along the stony, tree- and hedge-lined path, climbing another stile and keeping by a stream on the right. Turn right to cross a footbridge over the stream, turn left along the other bank, climb a stile and keep ahead to cross another footbridge over the River Cennen (D).

Turn right and almost immediately turn sharp left, at a footpath sign to Carreg Cennen, onto an attractive path which heads steadily uphill through the lovely, sloping Coed y Castell (Castle Wood) towards the castle, a grand finale to the walk. Continue past the castle entrance at the top and follow the path as it descends, turning right through a kissing-gate, on through another one and down through Castle Farm to return to the start. □

6 Ogmore Castle and Merthyr Mawr

Start: Ogmore Castle

Distance: 5 miles (8 km).
4 miles (6.5 km) if stepping-stones are used

Approximate time: 2½ hours (2 hours if using stepping-stones)

Parking: Car park at Ogmore Castle

Refreshments: Pub and farm café at Ogmore Castle, snacks at Ton Farm near Merthyr Mawr

Ordnance Survey maps: Landranger 170 (Vale of Glamorgan & Rhondda area), Pathfinder 1163, SS 87/96/97 (Bridgend (South) & Porthcawl)

General description From the picturesque ruins of Ogmore Castle the route crosses meadows lying between the Ewenny and Ogmore rivers to the equally picturesque village of Merthyr Mawr. Then a gentle climb across fields is followed by a descent through woodland on the edge of high dunes to the scanty remains of Candleston Castle. Finally there is a relaxing stroll along a lane to Merthyr Mawr before crossing the meadows again back to the start. This is an easy walk but expect some overgrown and indistinct paths north of Merthyr Mawr.

Ogmore Castle was built by the Normans to guard an important river crossing as they consolidated their control of the Vale of Glamorgan. The twelfth-century remains of the castle, comprising parts of the outer walls and the keep, occupy a delightful position above the River Ewenny not far from the coast.

There is a choice of routes from Ogmore Castle to Merthyr Mawr depending on whether you cross the River Ewenny by the stepping-stones or

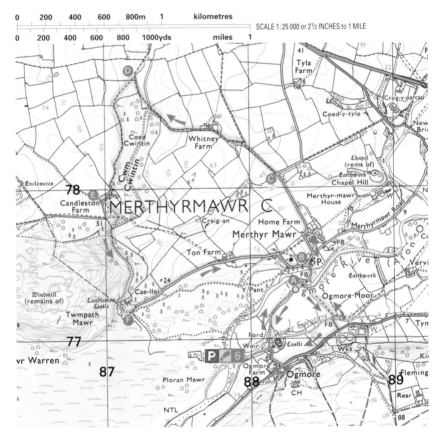

Stepping-stones over the River Ewenny at Ogmore

the footbridge. Using the footbridge route both ways adds about 1 mile (1.5 km) to the walk, or ½ mile (0.75 km) if using it in only one direction.

Either cross the stepping-stones over the River Ewenny and take the path ahead across meadow land, joining and keeping by a wall on the right, to reach a suspension footbridge over the River Ogmore. Or walk back up to the road, turn left, after ¼ mile (0.5 km) turn left beside a bus shelter, at a public footpath sign saying 'Merthyr Mawr Coastal Path' go through a metal-kissing gate, keep ahead to cross a footbridge over the River Ewenny and continue across meadows to climb a stone stile beside the suspension bridge.

Cross the bridge (**A**) and follow the road ahead into the idyllic village of Merthyr Mawr with its collection of widely spaced thatched cottages. At a T-junction turn right (**B**), then take the first turning on the left and walk along a lane for ¼ mile (0.5 km), heading uphill. Where the lane bends to the right (**C**), keep ahead along a gently ascending track to Whitney Farm. Go through two metal gates to the left of the farm and continue along a hedge-lined track. Where the track turns left to a gate, keep ahead along a grassy path partially enclosed by trees and hedges. The route now becomes more difficult to follow and the path may be muddy and overgrown in places. Later bear slightly right to continue along the left-hand edge of a field and by the right-hand edge of woodland, go through a metal gate, turn left to pass through a gap in a hedge-bank and turn right to head diagonally across a field – there is no visible path – making for a stile at the corner of a wood.

Climb the stile, bear right along the bottom right-hand edge of a field, by a line of trees and a wire fence on the right, and go through a gap in a wall into the next field. A few yards ahead, where the field edge turns right, turn sharp left (**D**) and head back to pass through another gap in the wall only a few yards above the previous one. Continue uphill across the field – again there is no visible path – making for the right-hand corner of a wood. Keep along the right-hand edge of the woodland as far as Candleston Farm, passing through two gates and finally turning left through a metal gate in a field corner.

Walk along a track, turning right towards the farm, turn left through a metal gate and turn right again to pass to the left of the farm buildings. At a left-hand bend ahead (**E**), turn sharply left along the lower of the two paths that bend left at this point. Follow the path downhill through trees, at a fork take the right-hand path and continue downhill, below the dunes of Merthyr-mawr Warren on the right, to reach Candleston Castle car park (**F**). Turn left to pass through the main entrance to the car park; the meagre ruins of what was a fifteenth-century fortified manor house lie just to the left on the edge of the dunes.

Keep ahead along a tree-lined lane for just under 1 mile (1.5 km) into Merthyr Mawr, passing the nineteenth-century church. In the village turn right (**B**) and retrace your steps to the start, via either the footbridge or the stepping-stones. ☐

7 Allt yr Esgair

Start:	Allt yr Esgair. Car park and picnic area off A40 ½ mile (0.75 km) south of Llansantffraed
Distance:	3½ miles (5.5 km)
Approximate time:	2 hours
Parking:	Car park at Allt yr Esgair
Refreshments:	None
Ordnance Survey maps:	Landranger 161 (Abergavenny & The Black Mountains), Outdoor Leisure 11 (Brecon Beacons – Central Area) and 13 (Brecon Beacons – Eastern area)

General description *Allt yr Esgair is a narrow, wooded ridge that lies between the Usk valley and Llangorse Lake. From its highest slopes there are extensive views and attractive woodland clothes its lower slopes. There is plenty of climbing but none is too steep or strenuous.*

Begin by going through a gate beside the car park, at a public bridleway sign to Allt yr Esgair, onto an enclosed track, and almost immediately turn left through a metal gate. Head diagonally uphill across two fields, go through a gate and continue uphill in the same direction to enter an attractive wooded area. All the way there are fine views through the trees to the left across the Usk valley to the Brecon Beacons. Go through a metal gate, continue through the woodland, go through another gate and climb steadily to reach a track.

Turn left along this lovely, grassy, fairly flat track which keeps along the left-hand edge of woodland; below on the left Llansantffraed church and the village of Talybont-on-Usk can be seen. Go through a metal gate and after a few yards turn right uphill, following the direction of a blue waymark, and almost immediately turn left onto a path running parallel to the track, just below it. Head steadily uphill, go through a metal gate and continue, now by a wire fence on the left. Cross a track and keep ahead to reach the ruined Paragon Tower, an early-nineteenth-century hunting-lodge.

At the end of the buildings climb a stile and continue along a narrow path that

The Brecon Beacons from Allt yr Esgair

winds through an area of gorse, trees, bracken and rough grass; the path, rather indistinct at times, descends slightly, keeping roughly in the same direction as before. When it emerges into an open meadow walk straight ahead across it, bearing right at the far end into trees. In front is a superb view of Llangorse Lake backed by Mynydd Llangorse.

On reaching a gate do not go through it but turn sharp right (**A**) and head uphill along a path through trees, keeping close to a wire fence and wall on the left. The path, sunken and enclosed in places, heads quite steeply uphill to reach the edge of a conifer plantation. Go through a gate and continue uphill along the right-hand edge of the plantation, by a wall on the left, to some large rocks at the top. Here is the finest view of all over the Usk valley to the Brecon Beacons.

Keep ahead, now descending, go through two metal gates and continue along a downhill track, lined at times by trees, to a third metal gate. Go through, walk down a hedge-lined path, take the first turning on the right (**B**), go through a gate and continue along another hedge-lined, enclosed path which bends to the right and heads down to a farm.

Just before reaching the farm turn sharp left, go through a gate to a T-junction of paths and turn right. A few yards ahead turn left (not sharply left through a metal gate) down an enclosed, stony, sunken, tree-lined path. Go through a gate and continue down to go through another gate to return to the start. ☐

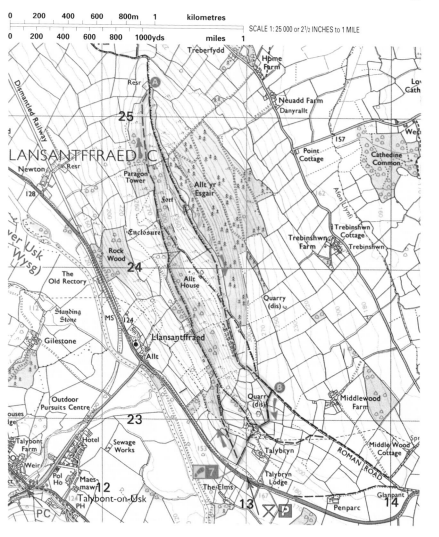

8 Ysgyryd Fawr

Start:	National park car park on B4521 between Abergavenny and Skenfrith
Distance:	3 miles (4.75 km)
Approximate time:	2 hours
Parking:	National park car park
Refreshments:	None
Ordnance Survey maps:	Landranger 161 (Abergavenny & The Black Mountains), Outdoor Leisure 13 (Brecon Beacons – Eastern area)

Approaching the summit of Ysgyryd Fawr

General description The distinctive bulk of Ysgyryd Fawr, alternatively called the Skirrid or Holy Mountain, lies to the north-east of Abergavenny and is the most easterly detached outlier of the Black Mountains. Its 'holy' connections derive from its shape: various legends claim that the cleft in its ridge was created either by Noah's Ark or at the time of the Crucifixion, but the more prosaic explanation is that it was the result of a massive landslip. The walk to its summit, a fairly easy climb initially through woodland and later along an open, grassy, narrow ridge, gives splendid views in all directions. Although it is possible to descend from the summit to a path that encircles the hill, the northern slopes are so steep that it is better to return by the same route, with the

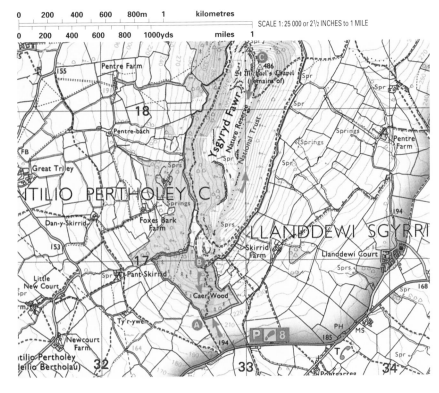

28

9 Cowbridge, Stalling Down and St Hilary

Start:	Cowbridge
Distance:	6½ miles (10.5 km)
Approximate time:	3½ hours
Parking:	Behind the town hall at Cowbridge
Refreshments:	Pubs and cafés at Cowbridge, pubs at Aberthin, pub at St Hilary
Ordnance Survey maps:	Landranger 170 (Vale of Glamorgan & Rhondda area), Pathfinders 1163, SS 87/96/97 (Bridgend (South) & Porthcawl) and 1164, ST 07 (Bonvilston)

opportunity to enjoy the fine views again from a different angle.

Start by climbing the stile at the side of the car park, at a public footpath sign to Skirrid Fawr, and walk along the track which soon bends to the right and climbs gently between wire fences to another stile. Climb that, keep ahead to where the path forks (**A**) and take the right-hand path, following a yellow waymark. The path climbs and winds steadily through delightful woodland, stepped in places and well waymarked. Climb a stile in a wall, here entering National Trust property (**B**), turn right alongside the wall for nearly 100 yards (91 m) and turn left onto a path that can be seen winding up the hillside.

The path continues quite steeply uphill, eventually emerging onto a small, open grassy area. Turn sharp right, shortly turn left to follow a well-worn path up to the ridge, and continue along the ridge to the triangulation pillar at the summit (**C**). The walk along this narrow, grassy ridge is most enjoyable, a gradual and easy climb with magnificent views on both sides. The finest views of all are from the summit (1,595 feet (486 m)): a great arc takes in Abergavenny, the Usk valley, Blorenge, the Sugar Loaf, the Black Mountains, and the more gentle countryside to the east looking towards the English border and the Wye and Monnow valleys. In the Middle Ages a chapel was built here for the pilgrims who were attracted by the hill's religious connections but it is virtually impossible to see any traces of it now.

From the summit retrace your steps to the start. □

General description *Starting from Cowbridge, this well-waymarked walk in the gentle, pastoral landscape of the Vale of Glamorgan uses a mixture of field paths, quiet lanes, farm tracks and woodland paths. The climb over Stalling Down is very gradual and gives fine views over the vale to the coast before descending into the thatched village of St Hilary.*

Refer to map overleaf.

Cowbridge, an ancient borough and the traditional capital of the Vale of Glamorgan, is a most attractive little town. The large church with its unusual octagonal tower and the substantial remains of the medieval walls, complete with a well-preserved gateway, on the south side of the town clearly indicate its former importance.

The walk starts in the car park behind the town hall. With your back to the town hall bear right, walk across the car park, and at a public footpath sign at the far end pick up a path that runs beside the little River Thaw. Just before reaching a footbridge over the river turn left along a tarmac path into a modern housing estate, take the first turning on the right and at the end of the houses keep ahead to pass under the Cowbridge bypass.

Climb a stile and continue along a track which bears left to a farm. Keeping to the left of the farm buildings go through a metal gate, climb the stile ahead and walk across a field to climb another stile. Bear left along the field edge, climb another stile and continue along the left-hand

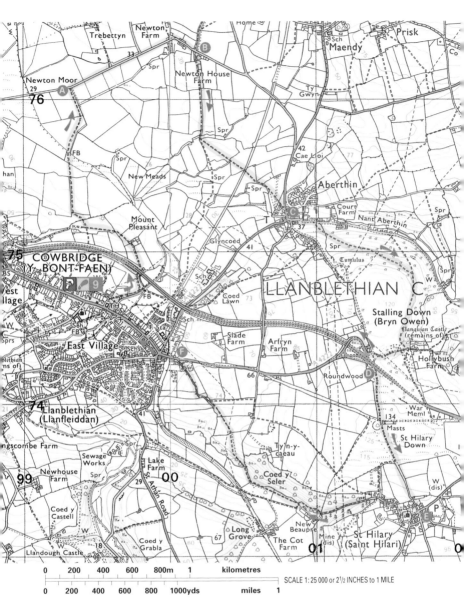

edge of a field, keeping parallel to a hedge on the left. About 100 yards (91 m) before reaching the end of this tapering field turn right and head across it to a metal kissing-gate in a hedge. Go through the gate, immediately climb a stile, bear left and walk across a field, parallel to a wire fence on the right, to turn right over a stile. Walk straight across the next field – there is no visible path – climb a stile, continue across the next field, cross a footbridge and keep ahead across the next field to cross another footbridge. Continue along the right-hand edge of a field, by a stream on the right, and where the stream bears

right keep straight ahead across the field corner to pass through a gap in a hedge. Continue across the next field to go through a gate onto a lane (**A**).

Turn right along the lane for nearly ¾ mile (1.25 km) and shortly after it bends right into the hamlet of Newton turn right (**B**) through a metal gate, at a public footpath sign, and walk along the track between farm buildings on the left and a wall on the right. Go through a succession of metal gates and continue along the track, between a hedge on the left and a wire fence on the right, to a stone stile at a public footpath sign. Climb the stile and keep along the left-hand edge of a field, go through a metal gate in the field corner and through another a few yards ahead and continue along a hedge-lined track.

Just before entering the next field turn left over a stile, bear left and head diagonally across a field, making for a yellow-waymarked post by a hedge gap on the far side. The rest of the walk is waymarked with regular 'Circular Walk' footpath signs and posts. Go through the hedge gap, continue in the same direction across the next field, go through a metal kissing-gate and walk across the next field to a stile in the corner. Climb it, keep ahead to go through another metal kissing-gate, continue along the right-hand edge of a field, by a hedge on the right, and follow the field edge at it curves to the right. Make for a kissing-gate on the far side of the field, go through it and walk along a track to the road in Aberthin.

Turn right and where the road bends right between the two village pubs turn left along Llanquian Road (**C**). Look out for a waymarked post and turn right here along a clear, sandy, uphill path through bracken which curves right over Stalling Down. On this section of the walk there are fine views over the gentle, pastoral vale; the monument that can be seen is in memory of the men of the Glamorgan Yeomanry who fell in the two world wars. At the end of a field bear left along a wide grassy track towards a farm and turn right along the farm drive which bends to the right to reach a road. Turn left, follow the road around a right-hand bend, turn left to cross a bridge over the A48 and on the other side turn left again to the main road.

Shortly bear right (**D**), at a public footpath sign, onto a grassy path that heads gently uphill through bushes and bracken. Pass to the right of a pair of masts, cross a track and continue along an enclosed track which, as it descends into St Hilary, gives striking views of the church tower below, beyond that Aberthaw power station and the Bristol Channel, and on the horizon the hills of Exmoor. On the edge of the village the track becomes a tarmac lane which continues to a crossroads (**E**). Turn right into this exceptionally picturesque village of old cottages – some of them thatched – a fine medieval church and a thatched inn. Follow the lane first around a right-hand bend beside the inn, then around a left-hand bend and head downhill.

The lane later continues as a rough downhill track through woodland and at the entrance to New Beaupre turn right, at a public footpath sign, along a path that heads up and shortly turns left to continue through woodland. The path bends left and descends to a stile; climb it and turn right along the right-hand edge of a field, by a wire fence bordering woodland on the right. Climb another stile, continue, still by the wood on the right, and where the field edge bends left keep ahead over a stile and bear slightly left to head up between trees into a field. Continue uphill straight across the middle of the field – there is no visible path – to climb a stile on the far side.

Continue across the next field, veering left to go through a hedge gap just to the right of the field corner, and keep in the same direction across the end of the next field, bearing left to climb a stile in the corner of it. Turn right along an enclosed, hedge- and tree-lined path which later continues as a tarmac path that descends between houses to a road (**F**). Turn left to return to the centre of Cowbridge. □

The thatched Bush Inn at St Hilary

10 Craig y Cilau and Llangattock

Start: Craig y Cilau. From
                     Llangattock take
                     road signposted to
                     Beaufort and park on
                     verge just beyond
                     cattle-grid about
                     1½ miles (2.5 km)
                     after canal bridge

Distance: 5½ miles (8.75 km).
                     Shorter version
                     4½ miles (7.25 km)

Approximate time: 3 hours (2½ hours
                     for shorter version)

Parking: On verge below
                     Craig y Cilau

Refreshments: Pub at Llangattock

Ordnance Survey   Landranger 161
maps: (Abergavenny & The
                     Black Mountains),
                     Outdoor Leisure 13
                     (Brecon Beacons –
                     Eastern area)

General description *Craig y Cilau forms part of the northern edge of Mynydd Llangatwg, a steep, dramatic limestone escarpment overlooking the Usk valley. Not only is it a fine viewpoint but it is of considerable botanical, geological and historic interest. The walk starts just below the escarpment and the first part of it is along field paths and quiet lanes, mostly through or along the edge of woodland, and includes a short but very attractive section along the towpath of the Monmouthshire and Brecon Canal and a visit to the village of Llangattock. Later there is a steep climb onto the escarpment, followed by a splendid walk across the face of it before the descent to return to the starting point. The shorter version of the walk omits the village of Llangattock.*

With your back to the cattle-grid turn right, at a public footpath sign to 'Coetgae Du and Cwm Onneu Farm', and head downhill to climb a stile. Continue downhill across a field, keeping parallel to a line of trees on the right, go through a metal gate in the bottom right-hand corner and follow a stony path through woodland. After emerging into a field bear left to keep parallel to its left-hand edge, which is bordered by woodland, descending steeply into a valley.

At the bottom, just before reaching a ford, turn right (**A**) along a track which climbs gently above the wooded valley on the left. Where the track peters out keep ahead along the left-hand edge of a succession of fields, by the woodland of Coed y Cilau on the left, climbing a series of stiles. Eventually go through a metal gate, continue along an enclosed track, and after passing through another metal gate the track curves first to the right and then to the left to Cilau Farm. At the farm turn right through a metal gate, walk through the farmyard, passing to the right of the farmhouse, and continue along a tarmac track. Where the track turns right climb a stile in front and keep ahead, parallel to the left-hand edge of a field. Climb another stile, bear right across the next field, making for a stile and public footpath sign on its right-hand edge, and climb the stile onto a lane. Turn left, cross the canal bridge (**B**) and turn right down to the canal.

*For the shorter version of the walk, omitting Llangattock, turn left here and walk along the towpath to the next bridge about 100 yards (91 m) ahead. Pass under it and turn left up to a lane, turning left to rejoin the full walk at (**E**).*

Turn right under the bridge and along the right bank of the canal for nearly ½ mile (0.75 km), as far as the next bridge. This is a delightful stretch of the Monmouthshire and Brecon Canal: it is tree-lined, tranquil and with some lovely views through gaps in trees on the right of Llangattock church, the Usk valley, Crickhowell and on the horizon the distinctive, flat top of Table Mountain.

At the bridge (**C**) turn right over a stone stile, at a public footpath sign, and turn right downhill along a lane, following it around a right-hand bend into Llangattock, an attractive village of narrow streets, old cottages and a solid-looking medieval church. The lane bends right by the church and continues through the village to a T-junction (**D**). Turn right along the road signposted to Beaufort and after ¼ mile (0.5 km) bear left at a fork in front of a chapel. Cross a canal bridge (**E**) and continue along the lane for another ¼ mile (0.5 km). In front looms the forbidding-looking escarpment of Craig y Cilau.

Where the lane bends left turn right (**F**) over a stile, at a public footpath sign, almost immediately following the direction of another public footpath sign to the left. Walk along a grassy path, by a hedge on the left; this was once part of a tramway that carried stone from the quarries on Mynydd Llangatwg to

Llangattock Wharf on the Monmouthshire and Brecon Canal. The path later becomes enclosed and continues through woodland. Go through a metal gate, keep ahead to go through another and continue along this attractive, partially tree-lined path. Soon after passing to the right of a cottage the path bears left to cross a stream and continues along the right-hand edge of a field to a stile at the foot of a steep incline. This incline was the means by which wagons loaded with limestone were lowered down the escarpment into the valley from where they were carried via the tramway to the canal.

Climb the stile and then climb the incline, which is in two parts. This is by far the most strenuous and tiring part of the walk. On reaching a flatter open area at the top of the first incline keep ahead for a few yards and then turn left to climb a second incline, slightly less steep and stony than the first one, turning sharp right at the top onto a track (**G**). Now comes the most scenic and one of the easiest parts of the walk along this broad, flat, well-surfaced track, also a former quarry tramway, as it contours across the face of the escarpment, with magnificent views to the right over the Usk valley,

Crickhowell, Table Mountain and the Black Mountains, and a spectacular view in front of the line of the curving escarpment. A notice says that you are entering Craig y Cilau National Nature Reserve, noted for its cave systems, rare flora and limestone woodland.

The track passes the entrance to the Eglwys Faen cave and follows the curve of the escarpment to the right. Keep a sharp look out for a yellow waymark and follow its direction to bear right off the track onto a narrow but clear path that descends below the escarpment, keeping roughly parallel with it, through rocks and trees – take care at this point – eventually emerging into a more open area of grass and fern.

Continue across a flattish area, bearing slightly left to keep to the left of a stream and the marshland of Waun Ddu. At times the winding path becomes indistinct but keep to the left of the stream all the while and pick your way between the rocks, making for the clear ascending path that can be seen ahead. Pass by another nature reserve sign, head uphill by a wire fence on the right and turn left to continue along a track, by a wall on the right, for the short distance back to the starting point. □

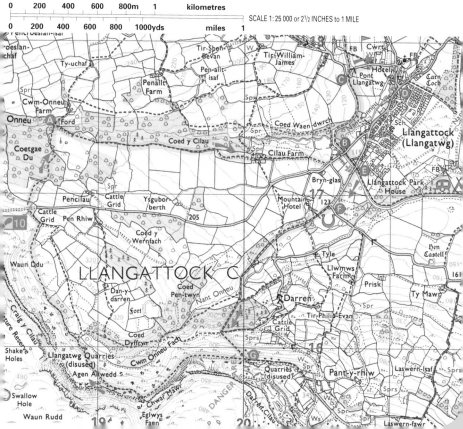

11 Ystradfellte and Sarn Helen

Start:	Ystradfellte. Shorter version starts at the Forestry Commission's Blaen Llia car park near point (**C**) about 2 miles (3.25 km) north of Ystradfellte
Distance:	6 miles (9.5 km). Shorter version 3 miles (4.75 km)
Approximate time:	3 hours (1½ hours for shorter version)
Parking:	Ystradfellte. For shorter version use Blaen Llia car park
Refreshments:	Pub at Ystradfellte
Ordnance Survey maps:	Landranger 160 (Brecon Beacons), Outdoor Leisure 11 (Brecon Beacons – Central area)

General description *This is a relatively undemanding walk through an austere, atmospheric limestone landscape with wide views over the empty expanses of Fforest Fawr. A particularly fine stretch along the Roman road of Sarn Helen to the south-west of Blaen Llia necessitates fording the River Neath (Nedd Fechan). If the river is running high and impossible to cross, which is likely after wet weather, an attractive alternative is to start from the Forestry Commission's Blaen Llia car park (near point (**C**)), walk down to the ford (point (**D**)) and retrace your steps.*

The isolated hamlet of Ystradfellte comprises little more than a church, a

The isolated standing stone of Maen Madoc

pub, a post office and a few houses, but it makes an excellent walking centre. From the car park turn sharp left along a tarmac track, go through a metal gate and head uphill. Where the tarmac track turns right to a farm continue uphill along an enclosed track, passing through two metal gates to emerge onto open moorland (**A**).

Ignoring a public footpath sign to the left, keep ahead, by a wall on the right, along a grassy path which veers slightly right across an austere, open landscape of grass, heather and isolated trees, littered with limestone boulders. Bear right to go through a metal gate and continue between the crags of Carnau Gwynion to another metal gate. Go through that to walk along a wide, walled, grassy track from which there are superb views ahead over mountains, moorland and forest. Climb a stile and follow the track to a road (**B**). Keep ahead along the road for ¾ mile (1.25 km), entering conifer plantations and passing Blaen Llia car park.

The shorter version of the walk starts from this car park, from where walkers should turn right along the road.

Just after the car park entrance there is a grand view ahead up the valley and to the right across the bare slopes of Fan Dringarth. About ¼ mile (0.5 km) past the car park turn sharp left (**C**) onto a broad track, go through a metal gate and follow the track through conifers. This track follows a well-preserved stretch of Sarn Helen, a Roman road that linked south and north Wales. Here it runs across the open moorlands of Fforest Fawr between the forts of Nidum (Neath) and Y Gaer, near Brecon. After going through another metal gate, leave the trees and continue across open moorland, with fine sweeping views across the valley of the River Neath, passing the isolated standing stone of Maen Madoc. It is probably of Celtic origin but the Romans later carved a Latin inscription on it. The track winds downhill, bending right through a metal gate to reach a ford over the River Neath (**D**).

If doing the shorter version of the walk, necessary if it is impossible to ford the river, retrace your steps from here back to Blaen Llia car park.

Cross the river and continue along Sarn Helen, going through a metal gate and heading gently uphill. A few yards in front of the next metal gate look out for and

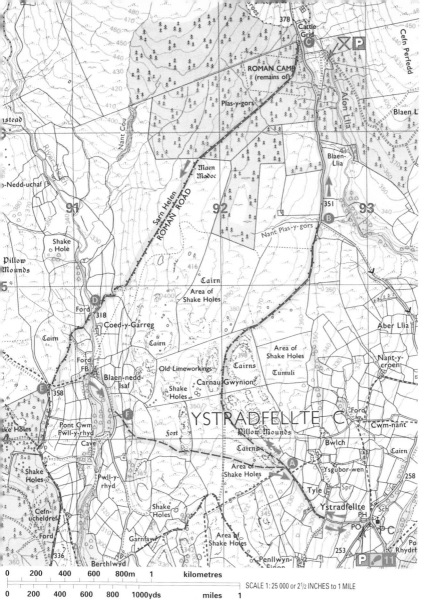

0	200	400	600	800m 1 kilometres
0	200	400	600	800 1000yds miles 1

SCALE 1:25 000 or 2½ INCHES to 1 MILE

turn left over a stile (**E**). Head downhill along the right-hand edge of a field, by a wall and fence on the right, go through a gate and continue, descending steeply to recross the River Neath, this time by a footbridge. Bear right to pass immediately to the right of a barn, go through a gate beside a second, older barn, keep ahead through the farmyard and turn right along a tarmac drive. Walk gently uphill and at a public footpath sign to Ystradfellte turn left over a stile (**F**).

Head diagonally uphill across a field to climb a stile in the top corner and continue in the same direction across the next field, bearing slightly left in the top corner through a small area of stunted trees. Continue once more across open grassy moorland, go over the brow of a hill, passing to the right of the remains of an Iron Age fort, and descend to a stile. Climb it, keep straight ahead across the moorland – there is no obvious path – heading downhill and making for a circular fence in front which encloses a shake hole, a depression in the limestone, one of many in this area.

Cross a track, pass to the left of the circular fence and bear slightly left – again there is no obvious path – keeping to the higher ground and aiming for a footpath sign at a wall corner (**A**). Here bear right through a metal gate and retrace your steps downhill to Ystradfellte. □

12 Llandovery and the River Towy

Start:	Llandovery
Distance:	6½ miles (10.5 km). Shorter version 5 miles (8 km)
Approximate time:	3½ hours (2½ hours for shorter version)
Parking:	Llandovery
Refreshments:	Pubs and cafés at Llandovery
Ordnance Survey maps:	Landranger 160 (Brecon Beacons), Pathfinder 1036, SN 63/73 (Llandovery)

General description *This walk around Llandovery in the pleasant countryside of the vale of Towy falls into two distinct halves: the first is a relaxing stroll across riverside meadows and the second is a modest climb over Allt Llwynywormwood, the wooded hillside to the south of the town. On the descent into Llandovery there are splendid views over both the Towy valley and the edge of the Brecon Beacons. The shorter version omits the second part of the walk.*

George Borrow, the nineteenth-century traveller and author of *Wild Wales,* described Llandovery as 'about the pleasantest little town in which I have halted' and pleasant is still a suitable adjective for this market town and former droving centre in the Towy valley. The large triangular market square has some dignified eighteenth- and nineteenth-century buildings and a town hall with a covered market. Overlooking the car park where the walk begins are the scanty remains of the thirteenth-century castle.

Walk back to the main street, turn right through Market Square and then left along Stone Street. Follow the road for nearly ¾ mile (1.25 km), crossing the A483 and passing under a railway bridge. Where the road bends slightly to the left turn right (**A**) over a stile and walk along the right-hand edge of a field, by a wire fence on the right.

Cross a footbridge, continue along a tree-lined path, and where the trees end bear slightly left off the main path, at a waymarked post, to climb a stile. Keep ahead along the bottom edge of steep-sided woodland on the right, by a wire fence and stream on the left, eventually crossing a footbridge over the stream.

Continue along the other bank for a few yards, turn left to cross another footbridge and bear right along the right-hand edge of a field. Go through a gap in the trees in the field corner and follow the direction of a yellow waymark to the left across the bottom edge of a sloping field to the next waymarked post. Continue along a track through woodland which passes through a metal gate and heads downhill. Look out for a stile, turn left over it and continue downhill across a field to climb another stile onto a road (**B**). Turn left, almost immediately turn right towards a bridge, but just in front of it turn left over a stile.

Walk along the right-hand edge of meadows, by the River Towy, climbing several stiles. After almost ½ mile (0.75 km) follow the edge of a meadow to the left and shortly turn right over a stile. Turn left along a narrow path between a stream on the right and a hedge and wire fence on the left, climb another stile and almost immediately turn right to cross a footbridge over the stream (**C**). Keep ahead towards a farm, climb a stile to the left of a metal gate, continue along a narrow path between a hedge on the left and a fence on the right, go up steps to climb another stile and keep ahead to join a tarmac farm drive. Bear left, go through a gate and bear right to cross another tarmac drive. Climb the stile immediately ahead, after a few yards climb another one and continue along the left-hand edge of a field, by a wire fence on the left, cutting a corner and eventually climbing a stile in the far narrow corner of the field.

Keep ahead along a broad, grassy, tree- and hedge-lined path, climb a stile and continue, shortly joining and keeping by a hedge on the left, slightly above the riverside meadow to the right. Climb a stile, bear slightly left to keep along the left-hand edge of the meadow, climb another stile and continue along a track to climb a third stile onto a road. Turn right towards a bridge but just before it turn left over a stile, descend some steps and head across to climb another stile.

Continue beside the river along the right-hand edge of first a meadow, then a sports field, and finally a golf-course. At the far, narrow end of the golf-course continue along a tree-lined path, passing under a railway bridge to a stile. Climb it, continue by the river for about another 100 yards (91 m) and then turn left (**D**) away from it to climb a stile beside a metal gate. Walk along a broad track, climb a stile and follow the track as it bends left towards farm buildings. Before the buildings look out for a stile beside a metal gate on the right, climb it and continue along a track for about 50 yards (46 m), between a hedge on the left and the Afon Brân on the right. Turn left over another stile and turn right along a broad farm track to a road (**E**).

For the shorter walk turn left along the road – there is a footpath beside it – for ³⁄₄ mile (1.25 km) back to Llandovery.

Turn right along the road, cross the bridge over the Afon Brân and take the turning on the left signposted to Myddfai. Head uphill and at a public footpath sign turn left (**F**) onto an uphill track which bears left to keep along the bottom edge of sloping woodland, by a wire fence on the left; the track later enters the woodland. At a fork in front of a sign saying 'Cwm Rhuddan clay pigeon shoot and horse riding circuit' take the left-hand, lower track, ignoring the stile ahead, to continue through woodland.

Climb a stile, immediately ford a narrow stream and continue to another stile. Climb that, leave the woodland and bear left off the track at a yellow-waymarked post, uphill across a field towards trees and gorse bushes at the top. Here turn left along a track, climb a stile and continue downhill, by a wire fence on the right, to a farm. Climb another stile, turn left to pass the abandoned farm buildings and in front of a house bear right, at a waymarked post, to head over the brow of the hill.

Descend to a stile, climb it and cross the next field diagonally to climb another stile in the far corner. Cross the next field in the same direction downhill, climb a stile on the edge of conifer woodland and follow the downhill track through trees. Bear right at a fork, keep ahead to climb a stile, bear left towards a farm, climb another stile, go in front of the farmhouse and continue along a concrete drive to a road (**G**). Turn left into Llandovery, crossing the Afon Brân, and at a crossroads turn left to return to the start. □

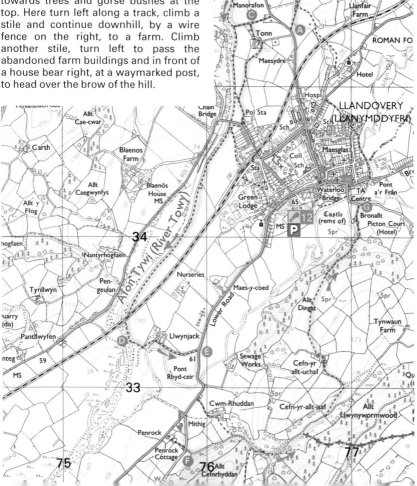

SCALE 1: 25 000 or 2½ INCHES to 1 MILE

13 Brecon, the River Honddu and Pen-y-crug

Start:	Brecon
Distance:	5 miles (8 km)
Approximate time:	2½ hours
Parking:	Brecon
Refreshments:	Pubs and cafés at Brecon
Ordnance Survey maps:	Landranger 160 (Brecon Beacons), Pathfinders 1038, SO 03/13 (Talgarth) and 1062, SO 02/12 (Brecon)

General description This walk falls into three distinct sections. An attractive stroll along the top edge of the steep-sided, thickly wooded valley of the River Honddu is followed by a stretch along quiet roads and lanes to the slopes of Pen-y-crug. Finally there is an easy climb over Pen-y-crug, from whose modest height of 1,088 feet (331 m) there are spectacular views over the town, the Usk valley and the Brecon Beacons, before the descent back into Brecon.

Brecon, the largest town in the national park and the main centre for it, has as fine a situation as any town in the country. On the north bank of the Usk at its confluence with the Honddu, it overlooks the major central peaks of the Beacons. The slight remains of its Norman castle, which was founded by Bernard de Newmarche in the early twelfth century and was the principal Norman stronghold in the area, are now mostly incorporated within the buildings of the Castle Hotel and overlook the meeting of the two rivers. In a

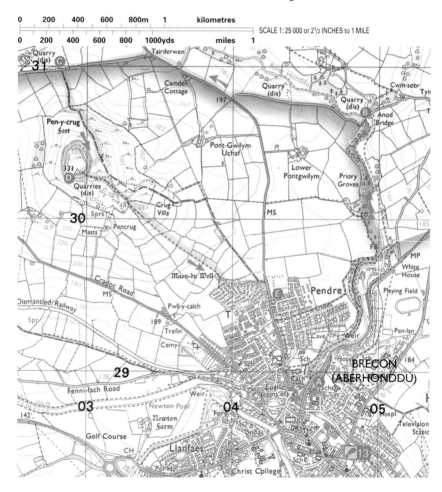

secluded position above the town stands Brecon Cathedral, formerly a Benedictine priory also founded by de Newmarche. Externally it is a plain, solid building whose massive central tower gives it an almost fortress-like appearance; in contrast the interior is light and elegant with a fourteenth-century nave and impressive thirteenth-century choir and lancet windows. It became a cathedral in 1923. The town centre still retains its medieval street pattern and the many Georgian buildings reflect Brecon's heyday as a fashionable social centre in the eighteenth century.

Start in Wellington Square in the centre of Brecon and walk along High Street Inferior, passing to the right of St Mary's Church. Bear right to continue along High Street Superior and about 50 yards (46 m) beyond the turning to Upper Chapel and Brecon Cathedral turn left (**A**) to cross a footbridge over the River Honddu onto a tarmac path.

The path bends to the right and heads uphill between walls. At the top bear right, at a public footpath sign, to continue along a clear path above the steep, wooded valley of the River Honddu, keeping just below the hedgeline on the left most of the time. This is a most attractive part of the walk through delightful woodland. At a T-junction of paths in front of a hedge turn right and continue, by a hedge on the left, along the top edge of the woods. Where the path forks at a public footpath sign a few yards ahead, keep ahead along the left-hand, upper path, still by a hedge on the left.

Look out for a public footpath sign to Llanddew, follow its direction to the right, cross a footbridge over a stream and head uphill to reach a fork. Take the left-hand path and continue above the valley, by a hedge on the left, as far as a stile on the edge of the woodland. Climb it, turn right, and head quite steeply downhill along the right-hand edge of a field to join the river. Keep along the pleasant, tree-lined bank of the Honddu as it curves left and climb a stile in the field corner onto a lane just to the left of Anod Bridge (**B**).

Turn left along the lane to a T-junction, turn right along the road for just under ½ mile (0.75 km) and at a junction turn left along the road signposted to Cradoc. Head gently uphill and just before the brow of the hill turn left (**C**), at a public bridleway sign, along an uphill, hedge-lined track which later narrows to a path and continues more steeply to a gate.

Go through onto the open hillside and continue along the path that contours along the side of the hill, curving gradually to the right and heading over the shoulder of Pen-y-crug. When you see the triangulation pillar on the summit to the right, detour off the path and head up to it (**D**) – it is encircled by the ramparts and ditches of an Iron Age hill fort – to enjoy the superb view over Brecon and the Usk valley with the line of the Beacons on the horizon.

From the triangulation pillar bear left along a grassy, downhill path to rejoin the main path at a waymarked post and bear right along it. Soon leave this path again by bearing left, when you see a yellow-waymarked stile just below on the left by a circle of trees and a public footpath sign for Pen-y-crug. Climb the stile, walk through the circle of trees and continue downhill, keeping parallel to a line of trees on the right, passing a waymarked post and heading down to another stile.

Climb it and continue downhill in a straight line across the middle of two fields, climbing yellow-waymarked stiles. After climbing the stile at the bottom of the last field another stile on the left gives access to Maen-du Well, a reconstructed medieval structure. The route continues straight ahead, passing through a gap in the trees in front onto a road and small parking area on the edge of a housing estate. Turn left along the road and follow it as it curves right down to a T-junction by a footpath sign to Maen-du Well.

Turn left for a few yards to the main road and turn right (**E**) to follow the road downhill, passing the west front of the cathedral, back to Brecon town centre. □

The Usk valley from Pen-y-crug

14 The head of the Dare valley

Start:	Dare Valley Country Park
Distance:	5 miles (8 km). Shorter version 3½ miles (5.5 km)
Approximate time:	3 hours (2 hours for shorter version)
Parking:	Dare Valley Country Park
Refreshments:	Café at country park visitors' centre
Ordnance Survey maps:	Landranger 170 (Vale of Glamorgan & Rhondda area), Pathfinder 1108, SN 80/90 (Hirwaun)

General description *Part of this walk at the head of the Dare valley, one of the former coal-mining valleys, is through what is called a post-industrial landscape. Some colliery headstocks have been retained as a symbol and there are remains of some spoil tips, but there is little other visual evidence of the previous mining activity. The walk encircles the head of the valley and there are spectacular views down the length of it, especially on the descent where the line of the Brecon Beacons can be seen on the horizon. Although the ascent is steep, the descent is easy and gradual. From the head of the valley the full walk continues across open grassy moorland to Lluest-wen reservoir at the head of the neighbouring valley of Rhondda Fach, an extension that is well worth while except in bad, especially misty, conditions when route finding could be difficult.*

In the early 1970s a massive programme of land reclamation took place in the upper Dare valley. Coal tips were levelled and landscaped, the river was rerouted, lakes and a cascade were created and thousands of trees were planted. The result was the transformation of an industrial eyesore into a highly attractive country park, enhanced by its industrial heritage and its dramatic setting at the head of the valley below steep rocky cliffs. A new and informative visitors' centre was opened in 1993.

From the visitors' centre turn right along the road and a few yards past the end of the buildings turn right through a kissing-gate onto a path. Bear left on joining another path a few yards ahead, follow it to a stile, climb it, walk through a car park and at the far end keep straight ahead along a path into trees.

The path heads down to join a tarmac path above a lake. Turn left along it, cross a footbridge by a cascade and keep ahead to a road. Turn left and where the road bends to the left a few yards ahead bear right to pass through a gap between a fence and trees; turn right a few yards ahead along a broad track. In front are fine, dramatic views of the head of the valley. On reaching a lake turn left over a footbridge, continue beside the lake, by a wire fence on the left, cross another footbridge at the far end and bear right across a parking and picnic area towards the headstocks of a former mine. Pass to the left of these and bear slightly left along a grassy path to a corner of a wire fence. A few yards further on turn left over a stile and continue along the left-hand edge of a small reservoir. To the right are some disused coal tips. Go through a metal gate, cross a footbridge, turn right to head gently uphill along a track and go through a gate onto a road.

Turn right and at the junction ahead turn sharp left (**A**) uphill, by a row of terraced cottages on the right. Where the road ends keep ahead along a track, passing to the right of farm buildings. Go through a gate, keep ahead along a grassy path, pass beside a metal gate and a few yards beyond it bear right to head steeply uphill along a fairly clear path. Make for a quarry and here bear left to join a track and continue uphill. After passing the end of the quarry keep ahead across grass and through bracken, bear left on joining another path and head uphill to a stile.

Climb it and continue uphill as the path bears left across the head of the valley. At a fork take the left-hand path, shortly crossing the infant River Dare – this is often dry – just above a waterfall. From here there is a spectacular view down the valley to the lakes of the country park, Aberdare town and the hills beyond. At a fork here take the right-hand path to

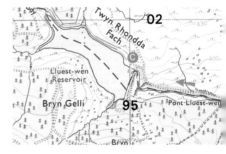

continue steadily uphill to a path junction by some rocks and a waymarked post. Turn left and after about 100 yards (91 m) reach another path junction by a white concrete marker-post (**B**).

*For the shorter walk bear left here and follow the directions after (**B**) below.*

Turn sharp right along a clear path that curves across open, windswept, grassy moorland between the head of the Dare valley and the head of the valley of Rhondda Fach, following the line of concrete marker-posts; this is part of the Coed Morgannwg Way. Later there are fine views to the left down Rhondda Fach. Eventually the path descends to a tarmac track by a bend. Turn right to follow the track for ½ mile (0.75 km), by the Rhondda Fach river and conifer plantations on the left, up to the dam of Lluest-wen reservoir (**C**).

Retrace your steps to the path junction where the shorter version of the walk diverged and turn right (**B**) to continue along the Coed Morgannwg Way, still curving around the head of the Dare valley above the rocks of Tarren y Bwllfa. There are more spectacular views down the valley with the line of the Brecon Beacons now clearly visible on the

Above the Dare valley

horizon. At a fork take the left-hand path, which begins a gradual and easy descent, to reach a stile. Climb it and continue downhill along a track, later curving left and heading more steeply downhill to a road (**D**). Turn right to return to the visitors' centre. □

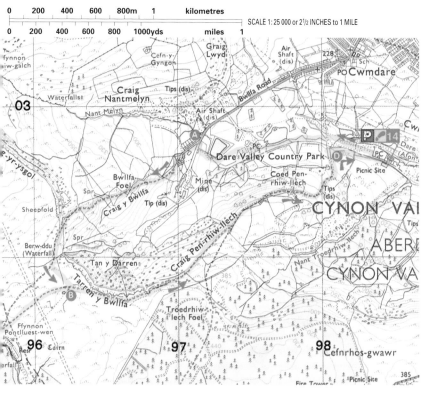

15 Mynydd Llangorse

Start:	Cockit Hill. Small parking area on bend at highest point of minor road 1¾ miles (3 km) east of Llangors village
Distance:	5½ miles (8.75 km)
Approximate time:	3 hours
Parking:	Parking area at Cockit Hill
Refreshments:	None
Ordnance Survey maps:	Landranger 161 (Abergavenny & The Black Mountains), Outdoor Leisure 13 (Brecon Beacons – Eastern area)

General description *This circuit of Mynydd Llangorse provides superb and ever-changing views for remarkably little effort. The only strenuous section is the steep climb between (**A**) and (**B**) out of the valley of Cwm Sorgwm onto the moorland plateau. The walk along the western slopes is particularly enjoyable; the path is tree lined at times and there are spectacular views over Llangorse Lake to the line of the Brecon Beacons.*

Start by heading southwards down the lane and after a few yards bear right onto a track which initially keeps parallel to the lane but later bears gradually right away from it. Follow the track along the side of Cwm Sorgwm and below the eastern slopes of Mynydd Llangorse for about 1¼ miles (2 km). About 100 yards (91 m) before reaching a metal gate, bear right (**A**) onto a grassy path that heads up the hillside, clips a fence corner and then continues more steeply uphill.

Follow the path first around a sharp right-hand bend, then around a left-hand bend, bear right to reach the top and continue along a grassy path through bracken and heather to a prominent cairn (**B**). The only strenuous part of the walk is now over and from the cairn there are superb views over the Black Mountains and the Usk valley.

Continue past the cairn to join another path and bear right along it to head over the open, breezy moorland on top of Mynydd Llangorse. Stay on the main path all the while, keeping right at two successive forks, to reach a crossroads of paths and tracks just in front of a small group of stunted trees, a rarity on this windswept plateau.

Here turn left onto a broad, grassy track and follow it across the moorland, gradually curving left and heading gently downhill to a crossroads by a fence corner and another cairn (**C**). Turn right to keep parallel to the fence on the left and where it ends continue ahead. Now there is the first of a series of superb and ever-changing views across Llangorse Lake and the Usk valley to the main peaks of the Brecon Beacons. The path curves to the right to contour along the western slopes of Mynydd Llangorse. Descend to go through a gate, continue, passing to the right of a cottage and on across a meadow, before descending again through conifer woodland. Bear right, go

Llangorse Lake and the Beacons from Mynydd Llangorse

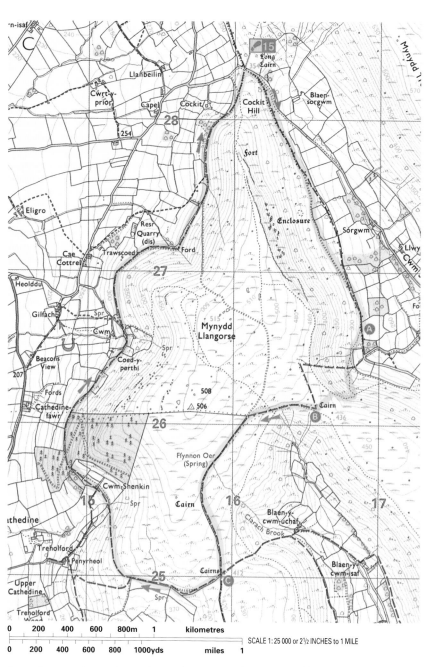

SCALE 1:25 000 or 2½ INCHES to 1 MILE

through a gate and continue down through the wood. Cross a track and keep ahead along an attractive tree-lined path, by the bottom edge of woodland and with a wire fence on the left.

Go through a gate to leave the wood and continue, keeping by a fence on the left for almost the remainder of the walk. The western slopes of Mynydd Llangorse are more wooded than those on the eastern side and this part of the walk makes a striking contrast with the early section.

Ford a stream and continue, taking the right-hand, upper path at the fork just in front. Ahead the view is now dominated by the distinctive bulk of Mynydd Troed. Eventually the path veers slightly right away from the fence to lead directly back to the starting point. □

16 Table Mountain

Start:	Crickhowell
Distance:	5 miles (8 km)
Approximate time:	2½ hours
Parking:	Crickhowell
Refreshments:	Pubs and cafés at Crickhowell
Ordnance Survey maps:	Landranger 161 (Abergavenny & The Black Mountains), Outdoor Leisure 13 (Brecon Beacons – Eastern area)

General description *It is easy to see how Crug Hywel, with its distinctive flat top, lying just to the north of Crickhowell, gets its nickname of Table Mountain. From Crickhowell the 1,481-foot (451 m) summit – crowned by an Iron Age fort and with a superb viewpoint – is reached via a mixture of lanes, farm tracks and field and moorland paths. The return is mostly along the side of a narrow, enclosed, wooded valley. Both the ascent and decent are gradual and relatively easy.*

The attractive little town of Crickhowell, with its many Georgian houses, gets its name from the mountain Crug Hywel. Narrow streets lead down from the town centre to the well-known, eighteenth-century stone bridge over the River Usk which has thirteen arches on one side but only twelve on the other. Of the thirteenth-century castle only the motte and a few walls remain, but the fourteenth-century church is an imposing building and unusual for this part of the country in having a spire, albeit a short one. Crickhowell's most famous son is the surveyor Sir George Everest, after whom the world's highest mountain is named.

Begin in the town centre and turn up Standard Street, which curves to the right and heads uphill. After ¼ mile (0.5 km) turn left along Great Oak Road (**A**), which is signposted to Grwynne Fechan, and follow the road uphill for just over ½ mile (0.75 km), making directly for the flat-topped Table Mountain in front. Where the road bends slightly right turn left through a metal gate (**B**), at a public footpath sign, and walk along a tarmac track towards a farm.

Go through a metal gate, continue through the farmyard and in front of the farmhouse turn right through another metal gate. Continue along the left-hand edge of a field by a hedge on the left, go through a metal gate in the field corner to a T-junction of paths and turn left along an

The old bridge at Crickhowell with Table Mountain in the background

enclosed, hedge-lined path, walking gently uphill to a stile. Climb it, continue along the right-hand edge of a field, climb another stile and head steadily uphill along the right-hand edge of the next field, by a wire fence and line of trees on the right, to climb another stile. Turn left in the direction of the yellow waymark, bear slightly right to climb a stile and continue along the right-hand edge of the next field, by a hedge on the right.

Climb a stile in the top corner and follow the direction of both the yellow waymark and a 'To the Mountain' sign to the right along a pleasant, tree-lined path, passing to the left of a farmhouse. The next stile admits you to the open moorland of Table Mountain. Bear slightly left to follow a clear, grassy path gently uphill between bracken over the lower slopes of the mountain, curving slightly left to a fork (**C**). Here bear left along the upper path to continue contouring along the side of the mountain, and at the highest point on the shoulder take the path to the left for a brief detour to the summit. Pass through the rocks that mark the ramparts of the Iron Age fort to reach the summit cairn (**D**), where the tremendous all-round view includes Crickhowell, the Usk valley, Mynydd Llangatwg, the Grwynne Fechan valley, the long ridge of Pen Cerrig-calch and in the distance the main Brecon Beacons ridge.

Return to the main path and turn left to continue around the slopes of the mountain. Where the main path bears right in front of a wall, keep ahead to join the wall and continue alongside it, following a path that meanders across the moorland, crossing several small streams and heading downhill. Eventually you reach a waymarked post; continue past it along a more rocky path to a sheepfold. Go through the metal gate in front and follow the direction of a footpath notice ahead to turn left (**E**).

Go through two metal gates in quick succession and continue along a path enclosed by walls. There is now a short awkward section of about 20 yards (18 m) along the bed of a stream – there are plenty of rocks to step on to keep your feet dry. After the stream bends right the route continues ahead along a distinct path across a narrow field towards woodland. On the edge of the trees turn left to ford a stream and turn right through a metal gate to follow a sunken path downhill along the left-hand edge of the narrow, steep-sided, wooded valley of Cwm Cumbeth to a gate. Go through and continue along the edge of this delightful

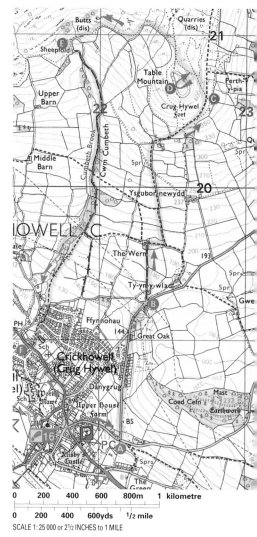

wooded valley, through several stiles, keeping more or less in a straight line and with views of Crickhowell below.

Eventually climb a stile to the right of a modern barn, bear left to climb another one and drop down to a lane. Turn left to a public footpath sign a few yards ahead and turn right through a gate to a modern housing area on the edge of Crickhowell. Cross a road and at a yellow waymark opposite follow a tarmac path downhill between houses. Cross another road, continue along the tarmac path between more houses and bear right along the road ahead, passing to the right of a school. Where the road ends keep ahead along a tarmac path down to the main road (**F**) and turn left to return to the start. □

17 Llanddeusant and Mynydd y Llan

Start:	Pont 'ar Wysg
Distance:	8 miles (12.75 km)
Approximate time:	4½ hours
Parking:	Forestry Commission's Glasfynydd Forest car park at Pont 'ar Wysg
Refreshments:	None
Ordnance Survey maps:	Landranger 160 (Brecon Beacons), Outdoor Leisure 12 (Brecon Beacons – Western area)

General description The region of the Black Mountain, the westernmost range of the Brecon Beacons National Park, is a true wilderness, a remote and largely empty area of wide horizons dominated by the bold and unmistakable profile of the Carmarthen Fans which are in sight for most of the route. This is an outstanding walk with superb views all the way and a tremendous feeling of spaciousness. Part of the route, however, is across open, featureless and pathless moorland where distant landmarks are essential for route finding; therefore in no circumstances attempt the walk in misty weather unless experienced in using a compass. There are likely to be some overgrown and muddy paths between Talsarn and Llanddeusant but although there is plenty of rough walking there are no steep or difficult climbs.

Turn left out of the car park and cross the bridge over the River Usk. The first 2½ miles (4 km) is along a straight road, the easiest and most straightforward part of the walk. All around are wide and striking views across open country; to the left across Mynydd y Llan are the Carmarthen Fans and to the right the smooth slopes of Fedw Fawr. At first you can walk beside the road across unfenced common but later, after a cattle-grid, the road becomes fenced.

At the collection of cottages that comprise the hamlet of Talsarn turn left through a gate (**A**), just after passing a chapel, and walk along a hedge-lined, enclosed track which soon bends left and heads downhill to end at a metal gate. Bear right here to continue down a much narrower, sunken, hedge- and tree-

enclosed path – this is likely to be a muddy, overgrown and difficult section – to a gate. Go through, keep ahead for a few yards and then turn right to continue down another sunken path. Again this could be muddy and overgrown and it may be easier to walk along the field edges parallel to it, although later the path improves as it becomes tree lined and descends to a stile at the bottom of a lovely wooded gorge.

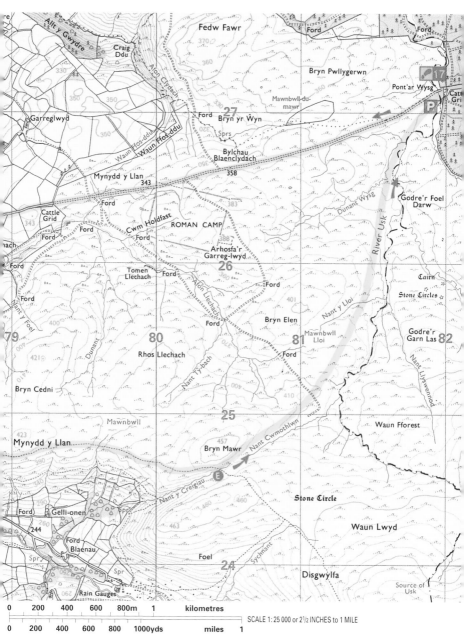

Climb the stile, cross a footbridge over the Afon Llechach and turn right to continue along a path above the river, curving left to climb another stile near Aberdyfnant Farm. Continue up to pass to the left of the farmhouse and turn left along a rough tarmac track which heads uphill and bends to the right. There is now a delightful stretch of walking along a flat, partially tree-lined track with pleasant views to the right over rolling countryside.

The track descends to a narrow lane (**B**). Follow it for ¼ mile (0.5 km), heading uphill into Llanddeusant and keeping to the left of the youth hostel and the small, plain, remote, medieval church to reach a T-junction (**C**).

Turn left along the lane signposted to Llyn y Fan, and where it bears slightly right bear left to climb a stile and walk along a grassy track enclosed by trees and hedge-banks. Cross a track, continue

The bold profile of the Carmarthen Fans

gently uphill to climb a stile and just ahead is a footpath sign (**D**). Turn right here in the direction of the white arrow onto an 'Advised Path' and walk along the right-hand edge of a field, by a line of trees and the hedge-bank of a parallel sunken track to the right. Head up to a stile, climb it and continue gently uphill to climb another stile onto open, grassy moorland.

Now comes the most scenic and exhilarating part of the walk as you continue along an uphill, grassy path over the lower slopes of Mynydd y Llan. All the way there are extensive, unhindered views across the smooth, open, grassy moorlands, especially to the right to the dramatic, forbidding-looking escarpment of the Carmarthen Fans, Bannau Sir Gaer and Fan Brycheiniog. Keep more or less in a straight line above the valley of the Afon Sychlwch on the right and after 1¼ miles (2 km) the path descends gently

into a shallow valley and bears right across its head.

At this point do not follow the path to the right but keep ahead (**E**) below the gentle slopes of Bryn Mawr on the left and above another shallow valley on the right. For most of the rest of the way there is no obvious path but the walking is relatively easy and there are no route-finding problems provided that conditions are clear. Follow the course of the valley on the right, curving gradually to the left across this pathless moorland and heading all the time towards the edge of the conifer forest and the Usk reservoir which can be seen in the distance. As you proceed, a winding stream – the infant River Usk – and later the road walked along at the start come into view.

Finally, pick up a distinct path which keeps by the left bank of the River Usk, ford a stream and continue to the road. Turn right over the bridge to return to the car park. □

18 Llantwit Major and the heritage coast

Start:	Llantwit Major
Distance:	8 miles (12.75 km). Shorter version 4½ miles (7.25 km)
Approximate time:	4 hours (2½ hours for shorter version)
Parking:	Llantwit Major
Refreshments:	Pubs and cafés at Llantwit Major, beach café at Cwm Col-huw
Ordnance Survey maps:	Landranger 170 (Vale of Glamorgan & Rhondda area), Pathfinder 1163, SS 87/96/97 (Bridgend (South) and Porthcawl)

General description Llantwit Major is situated in a shallow valley about 1 mile (1.5 km) inland and the walk begins by heading across fields to the sea and then continues along a particularly attractive section of the Glamorgan Heritage Coast. After nearly 1½ miles (2.5 km) the shorter route turns inland to return to the start but the full walk continues along the coast, passing through some delightful woodland, to the lighthouses at Nash Point. It then retraces this section before heading back to Llantwit Major. There are several ascents and descents but none are particularly strenuous.

Refer to map overleaf.

With its narrow winding streets and alleys and widely scattered stone cottages, Llantwit Major is one of the most attractive small towns in Wales. It also has a fascinating history. Its Welsh name is Llanilltud Fawr (Great Church of St Illtud) and the Celtic monastery that St Illtud founded here in the fifth century became a major centre of learning and missionary activity, virtually a Dark Age university. Nothing survives of this monastery and the only visible evidence of what must have been a flourishing community is the collection of carved stone crosses in St Illtud's Church.

The church is unusual and complex, really two churches in one separated by the tall, slim, central tower. The western (or Old) church is a fifteenth-century rebuilding of the original Norman parish church, with a ruined thirteenth-century Galilee chapel at its west end. The eastern (or Monastic) church was added in the thirteenth century. As well as the Celtic crosses there are some fine monuments and medieval murals inside. Other historic buildings in the town include a fifteenth-century town hall, a tithe barn, an old gatehouse and a circular dovecote.

The walk begins in the square in front of the town hall. Turn towards the church and walk down Burial Lane, passing to the left of the church. Cross a small river and

The Glamorgan Heritage Coast near Cwm Col-huw

49

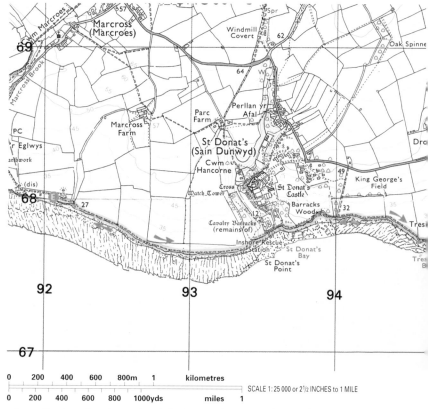

where the lane bends to the right keep ahead up steps and at the top turn left along a track in front of cottages (**A**). After a few yards turn right over a stone stile – ahead is the dovecote – turn left, keep along the left-hand edge of a field, by a wall on the left, and climb a stile in the bottom corner. Keep ahead by the wall on the left, descend steps into a farmyard and walk along a drive to a lane.

Turn right and shortly after passing Colhugh Park on the right turn left in front of a garage, at a yellow waymark, onto a very narrow path, between a wire fence on the left and a wall on the right. Descend to cross a footbridge over a stream, follow the path as it bends first to the right and then to the left, climb a stile and keep ahead to climb another one onto a road. Turn right along the road and just after a right-hand bend turn left along a broad tarmac track (**B**) at public footpath and Glamorgan Heritage Coast signs. The track curves right to pass to the left of farm buildings. Go through a gap to the side of a metal gate and continue along what is now a rough track. Climb a stile to the left of another metal gate, continue gently uphill along a hedge-lined track and look out for a public footpath sign;

here continue along a narrow path between fields to join the coast path (**C**).

Turn right onto it to walk along an attractive stretch of coast, with fine views to the right over the gentle vale and to the left across the Bristol Channel to the hills of Exmoor, and with superb cliff scenery ahead looking towards St Donat's Point and the lighthouse beyond. The walking is easy with a good, clear path, a number of stone stiles to negotiate and several series of steps by which you descend into bays and then climb up out of them.

Initially head along to Cwm Col-huw, passing the Iron Age enclosure of Castle Ditches, and zigzag down to the beach. Head up the other side to continue to Tresilian Bay, just before descending into it meeting a wall on the right with a stone stile in it (**D**).

For the shorter version of the walk turn right over the stile and follow the directions after (D) below.

Continue along the coast path, soon descending into Tresilian Bay and walking across the pebbly beach to climb cliffs on the other side. Continue towards St Donat's Bay, entering attractive

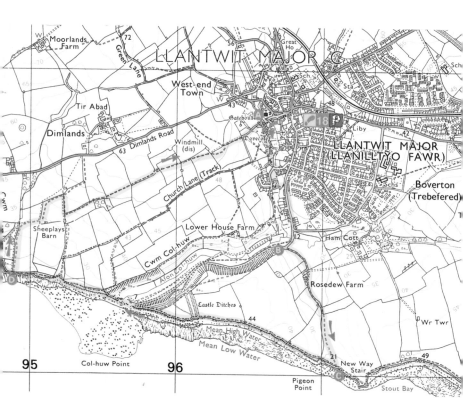

woodland, descend some steps and at a fork do not continue ahead down to the beach but turn right up more steps. Some of the buildings of St Donat's Castle, a modernised medieval fortress now housing the international Atlantic College, can just be seen to the right. Continue along the cliff top, descend to St Donat's Bay, walk across a concrete promenade in front of college buildings and climb up again through more beautiful woodland to emerge onto the open cliff top. There is now a lovely stretch of clifftop walking as far as the lighthouses (**E**). From here retrace your steps to the stone stile just beyond Tresilian Bay and turn left over it (**D**).

Walk along a path between a wire fence on the left and a wall on the right, climb a stile and continue by the wall on the right, later alongside the edge of woodland on the left. Climb some steps, turn right over a stone stile in the wall, walk straight across the field ahead and climb a stone stile just in front of the ruins of a barn. Turn left at the ruins along the edge of the field, turn right along a line of trees to the corner of the field and then turn right again alongside a hedge. Look for a waymarked stone stile on the left, climb it

and follow a path straight across the next field, in the Llantwit Major direction, making for the left side of a small group of trees. Climb another stone stile and bear right along the right-hand edge of a field by woodland on the right. Where the edge of the woodland turns right bear slightly left and head across the field. Climb a stile and continue along the right-hand edge of the next field, by a hedge on the right.

At the end of the field turn left to follow the field corner for a few yards, turn right over a stone stile and keep ahead to climb another stile. The houses of Llantwit Major can now be seen ahead. Continue across the next field, climb a stone stile, keep along the left-hand edge of the next field, climb another stone stile and bear slightly right away from the hedge on the left to cross the next field to a stile. Climb it, continue along the right-hand edge of a field by a hedge and wire fence on the right, climb a stone stile, keep ahead to climb another one and continue along a hedge-lined path.

The path later becomes a tarmac drive. Follow it to a T-junction, turn right and after a few yards turn left (**A**) down steps and follow the lane ahead up past the church to return to the start. ☐

19 Mynydd Illtud and Cefn Llechid

Start:	Mynydd Illtud. Brecon Beacons Mountain Centre 1½ miles (2.5 km) west of Libanus
Distance:	7½ miles (12 km)
Approximate time:	4 hours
Parking:	Brecon Beacons Mountain Centre at Mynydd Illtud
Refreshments:	Café at Brecon Beacons Mountain Centre
Ordnance Survey maps:	Landranger 160 (Brecon Beacons), Outdoor Leisure 11 (Brecon Beacons – Central area)

General description *From the open, spacious common land of Mynydd Illtud at the start and finish of the walk there are splendid views of the main ridge of the Brecon Beacons, and there are more open and extensive views from the slopes of Cefn Llechid, especially over the Usk valley. As a contrast there is the pleasant wooded valley of Cwm Camlais and easy and enjoyable walking along a wide drove road. This walk provides varied scenery and grand views for relatively little effort as there are no steep climbs or difficult terrain.*

The Brecon Beacons Mountain Centre, opened in 1966, is situated 1,100 feet (335 m) up on Mynydd Illtud, a large area of open common with grand panoramic views over the mountains. Begin by turning left out of the entrance along the road and at a T-junction leave the road and continue along a grassy track which keeps along the edge of the rather marshy common, near a wire fence and line of trees on the left. After ¾ mile (1.25 km), at a stile and public footpath sign on the left, turn right (**A**) along a broad, grassy track. This heads across the common in a north-westerly direction, between the two marshy areas of Traeth Mawr and Traeth Bach, to reach a road just to the right of a large pool (**B**).
  Cross the road, continue along the broad, grassy, enclosed track opposite – it is likely that this was an old drove road – and after nearly ½ mile (0.75 km) take the first turning on the left (**C**). Go through a

metal gate, head downhill along a hedge-lined, enclosed path, pass through another metal gate and continue down to a lane. Turn left along this narrow, winding lane for ¾ mile (1.25 km), following it around several sharp bends to reach the A4215.
  A few yards before the road turn right (**D**) through a gate onto a sunken path between hedge-banks and follow it gently uphill through a series of gates and stiles, eventually emerging onto the open, windswept Cefn Llechid Common. Continue along a grassy path through bracken, enjoying the extensive all-round views. On the skyline to the left the triangulation pillar marks the highest point on the common (1,314 feet (400 m)); it is worth a brief detour for the magnificent views. After passing several pools the route starts to descend, by a hedge-bank and wire fence on the right, with superb views ahead over the Usk valley.
  Go through a metal gate a few yards to the left of a fence corner and continue

quite steeply downhill along a sunken path, by a wire fence on the right, passing through a succession of gates and stiles to reach a narrow lane (**E**). Turn right along it for ½ mile (0.75 km), heading downhill, and where the lane bends left in front of Cwm-Camlais-uchaf Farm (**F**) keep ahead through the farmyard, bearing right through a metal gate at the far end to continue along a winding track. The track soon joins the lovely, tree-lined stream of Cwm Camlais which rushes over rocks and small falls. Turn left over a footbridge where the stream divides, bear right and head across to join an enclosed path. Bear left to follow this path uphill through woodland above the valley of Cwm Camlais-fach. Go through a metal gate and turn right to continue along an enclosed path between hedge-banks.

A few yards after the hedge-banks peter out look out for where the sunken enclosed path reappears on the left and follow it uphill to a gate on the edge of a plantation. Go through the gate to walk along the right inside edge of the

The Brecon Beacons from Mynydd Illtud

plantation, by a wire fence on the right, and just before reaching the corner of it turn right through another gate to continue along an uphill sunken path. Later the path levels out and continues as a wide, green, tree-lined enclosed track – the old drove road again; follow it through a series of gates and stiles, later picking up part of the outward route and continuing to the road (**B**). This is easy and most enjoyable walking, with the magnificent panorama of the Brecon Beacons spread out ahead all the while.

Leave the outward route at the road by turning left along it across Illtud Common and after ¾ mile (1.25 km) turn right along a lane signposted to the mountain centre. Follow it back to the start, passing to the left of the ruined church of Llanilltyd. ☐

| 0 | 200 | 400 | 600 | 800m | 1 | kilometre |

| 0 | 200 | 400 | 600yds | ½ mile |

SCALE 1:25 000 or 2½ INCHES to 1 MILE

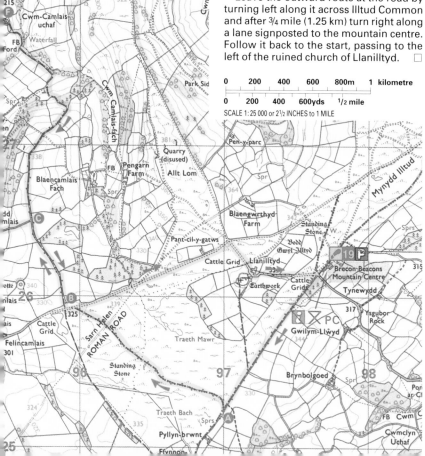

20 Hay Bluff and Twmpa

Start:	Hay Bluff. Car park beside stone circle on minor road between Hay-on-Wye and Abergavenny
Distance:	5½ miles (8.75 km)
Approximate time:	3 hours
Parking:	Car park at Hay Bluff
Refreshments:	None
Ordnance Survey maps:	Landranger 161 (Abergavenny & The Black Mountains), Outdoor Leisure 13 (Brecon Beacons – Eastern area)

General description The adjacent open expanses of Hay Bluff and Twmpa – the alternative name for the latter is Lord Hereford's Knob – are the most northerly peaks of the Black Mountains and from them there are extensive views of the long ridges of the mountains and over the Wye Valley to the hills of mid Wales. The walk involves two ascents: the first to the summit of Hay Bluff (2,220 feet (677 m)) is steep, the second to the summit of Twmpa (2,263 feet (689 m)) is easier and more gradual. It is best to choose a fine, clear day for this walk, to enjoy the grand views to the full and because otherwise route finding in such open terrain could be difficult.

From the car park and stone circle cross the road and head uphill across grass to the summit of Hay Bluff which lies abruptly ahead. It is a steep climb and various paths give the choice of either tackling it head on or contouring around. At the top make for the triangulation pillar (**A**) from which the views over the Black Mountains, Brecon Beacons, Wye Valley and hills of mid Wales are magnificent. Here turn right along a track that keeps along the edge of the escarpment of Ffynnon y Parc, heading towards the prominent steep face of Twmpa. The track eventually descends to the road and parking area at Gospel Pass (**B**), a narrow, ancient routeway over the mountains.

Cross over and take the obvious grassy track ahead that leads steadily up to the summit of Twmpa. Near the top the path passes between two cairns and continues to a third one which marks the summit,

The glorious open view from the summit of Twmpa

54

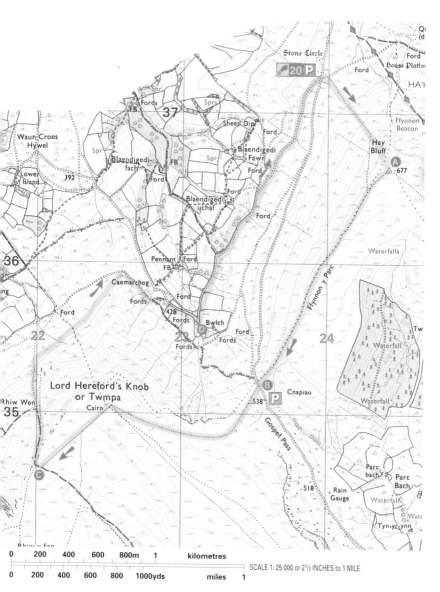

another superb viewpoint. From here continue along the edge of the escarpment, bearing slightly left and gently descending. Later the broad, grassy path levels out; follow it almost to the rim of the chasm ahead.

Turn right here (**C**) onto a rocky path which heads steeply downhill along the right-hand edge of the chasm, curving slightly right. After the steepest part of the descent ford a small stream and follow the clear path ahead across open grassland. The path descends more steeply again, passes a group of trees and continues below the slopes of Twmpa, curving gradually right all the while.

Later you join a wider path, bearing right and still keeping below the curving slopes of Twmpa. From here there are particularly dramatic views of Twmpa on the right and the long ridge of Hay Bluff ahead.

On joining a narrow lane turn right along it through a pleasant area of trees, ford two streams at a left-hand bend (**D**) and follow the lane for just over 1 mile (1.5 km) back to the start. This is a delightful, unspoilt, old-fashioned country lane which appears to be used more by walkers and riders than vehicles; it heads gently uphill across open country below Hay Bluff.

21 The vale of Ewyas

Start:	Llanthony Priory
Distance:	6 miles (9.5 km)
Approximate time:	3 hours
Parking:	Car park at Llanthony Priory
Refreshments:	Hotel at Llanthony Priory, pub at Llanthony
Ordnance Survey maps:	Landranger 161 (Abergavenny & The Black Mountains), Outdoor Leisure 13 (Brecon Beacons – Eastern area)

General description *The vale of Ewyas, a narrow, remote, steep-sided valley on the eastern edge of the Black Mountains, provides a romantic, secluded setting for the ruins of Llanthony Priory. Initially the walk follows a pleasant track northwards along the bottom of the valley before turning westwards to cross the River Honddu and climb onto open moorland. A delightful ramble follows, along the western slopes of the valley to Bal Bach, a fine viewpoint over both the vale of Ewyas and the neighbouring Grwyne Fawr valley. On the final descent the priory ruins are in sight most of the time. This highly scenic and quite energetic walk is best done on a fine day as in misty conditions route finding on the open moorland stretch could be difficult.*

The austere-looking ruins of Llanthony Priory perfectly match their setting in the peaceful, lonely vale of Ewyas enclosed by the bare slopes of the Black Mountains.

Llanthony Priory, deep in the vale of Ewyas

The Augustinian priory was founded in the early twelfth century and much of the late twelfth- and early-thirteenth-century church survives, notably the west front, the north arcade of the nave, the central tower and parts of the east end. Little remains of the domestic buildings, although the small parish church nearby incorporates the monks' infirmary. Uniquely, the south-west tower of the priory church is now part of the Abbey Hotel, surely one of the most unusually sited hotels in the country.

Leave the car park by walking between the priory ruins on the right and the church on the left. Climb a stile straight ahead and, ignoring the direction of a waymark to the right, continue across the field, making for a wire fence on the left. Climb a stile to the left of a barn – formerly the priory gatehouse – onto a road and bear right along it, passing the Half Moon Inn. Where the road bears left to Capel-y-ffyn, keep straight ahead (**A**) along a narrow, tarmac, enclosed lane, an old routeway that has remained 'unimproved'. After passing through a gate the lane becomes a tree-lined path, which may be muddy in places, and after the next gate it reverts to being a tarmac lane. In front there are lovely views looking towards the head of the valley.

At a public footpath sign to Hay Road turn left through a metal gate and head downhill along the left-hand edge of the field, by a wire fence bordering a stream on the left, later bearing right away from the field edge and going through a gap in a line of trees. Continue down, climb a stile and keep alongside the River Honddu, turning left over a footbridge. Climb a stile a few yards ahead, head across a field to climb another and continue up to the road.

Turn right and after a few yards, where the road bears slightly right, turn left (**B**) up some steps, climb a stile and head uphill along the left-hand edge of a field, by a wooded gully and stream on the left. Near the top of the field turn left through a metal gate, pass to the right of a farm, but do not enter the field in front. Instead turn right through a metal gate to continue uphill along the left-hand edge of a field, by a wire fence on the left. At the top climb a stile and turn left (**C**) to keep alongside a wire fence on the left, soon picking up a clear path which can be seen a few yards to the right. This path winds along the bottom edge of open moorland, keeping roughly parallel with the wire fence on the left. There are superb views over the valley and at times the ruins of Llanthony Priory can be glimpsed.

Where the path forks above a farm building, take the right-hand, upper path which heads away from the wire fence to join a wider, clearer path. Bear left along it, go through a metal gate and keep ahead to pass through another one. The path now starts to climb and becomes more rocky as first it bends right above the edge of a steep valley, and then it bears left across the head of the valley to continue across the lovely, open, heathery moorland on the western slopes of the vale of Ewyas.

Make for the cairn that can be seen on the skyline ahead; this is Bal Bach where there is a junction of tracks and paths and a view to the right over the forested Grwyne Fawr valley (**D**). Here turn left downhill along a broad, well-used path. At a fork take the right-hand path, shortly turning right and heading downhill along the left-hand side of the narrow, steep-sided valley of Cwm Bwchel. Be careful as the path is steep and rocky. As it descends there are glorious views of the priory ruins in front. At a footpath sign keep ahead in the Llanthony direction, climb a stile and continue downhill to climb another. Keep ahead, climb a stile to the left of a farm, continue along an enclosed path for 50 yards (46 m), climb another stile and keep along the right-hand edge of a field, by a wire fence on the right. Go through a gap in a line of trees and continue down to a stile. Climb it, turn right, climb another and cross a footbridge over a stream.

Turn left to follow the stream down to a stile, climb it, keep ahead to climb another and turn left along the field edge by the River Honddu down to one more stile. Turn left over it, cross an iron footbridge over the river and turn right along a track through a farmyard to a road. Cross the road and follow the lane opposite back to the priory. □

0   200   400   600   800m   1 kilometre

0   200   400   600yds   1/2 mile

SCALE 1: 25 000 or 2½ INCHES to 1 MILE

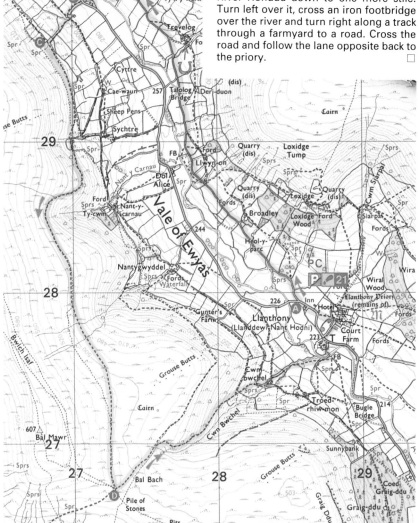

22 Grwyne Fawr valley and Crug Mawr

Start:	Ffawyddog
Distance:	7½ miles (12 km)
Approximate time:	4 hours
Parking:	Forestry Commission's Mynydd Du car park at Ffawyddog
Refreshments:	None
Ordnance Survey maps:	Landranger 161 (Abergavenny & The Black Mountains), Outdoor Leisure 13 (Brecon Beacons – Eastern area)

General description *The Grwyne Fawr valley is one of a series of long, narrow, parallel valleys that separate the ridges of the Black Mountains. The walk begins by heading uphill through the conifers of Mynydd Du Forest on the western side of the valley, emerging onto open moorland to reach the grand viewpoint of Crug Mawr (1,805 feet (550 m)). A descent to the delightful, secluded Partrishow church is followed by a high-level return route along the eastern side of the valley. Forest, moorland, wooded valley and extensive views all combine to create a most varied and satisfying walk, and although there is some climbing none of it is steep or strenuous.*

Leave the car park, cross the bridge (Pont Cadwgan) onto the road and take the forest track opposite which bears left and climbs steadily. Follow the track around a right-hand curve, keep ahead to a crossroads of tracks and bear left to continue along a winding track through a pleasant area of mixed woodland. Go through a gate, keep ahead to a farm, turn left at the end of the farm buildings, by a public bridleway sign, and continue between trees to a gate on the edge of the forest.

Here turn right (**A**) onto a path that climbs initially alongside the edge of the forest and later continues through the conifers. Keep ahead all the while along this waymarked path, crossing two forest tracks, and eventually go through a gate on the edge of the forest, emerging onto open moorland (**B**). Turn left onto a path that runs along the forest edge to the corner of the plantation, from where a triangulation pillar can be seen ahead on

the summit of Crug Mawr. A path heads towards it across the heathery moorland, ascending gently. From the summit (**C**) there is a magnificent panoramic view that includes the Sugar Loaf, Ysgyryd Fawr, the Grwyne Fawr valley, the western ridges of the Black Mountains, the Usk valley and the main Brecon Beacons beyond.

Retrace your steps to the corner of the forest, bear right and follow a path that winds downhill, keeping roughly parallel to the edge of the trees and later dipping below them. Where the path levels out pick up and continue along a pleasant, grassy track that curves to the right, following the bottom edge of Crug Mawr. Go through a gate, head down an enclosed, stony track to a lane, bear right and follow it downhill around some sharp bends to Partrishow church, turning left (**D**) into the churchyard. This is a delightful, unspoilt, secluded church in a lovely, remote mountain setting, and is particularly noted for its superb fifteenth-century carved oak screen. It also has a medieval painting of a skeleton on the west wall of the nave and a parish chest hewn from a solid tree trunk.

Pass to the right of the church, go through a gate at the far end of the churchyard and continue across a sloping field. Bear right on joining a track, follow it around a sharp right-hand bend and continue down to the attractive fifteenth-century buildings of Tyn-y-llwyn Farm. Turn left, passing to the right of the farmhouse, go through the left-hand one of two metal gates ahead and walk across a field to a stile. Climb it, bear right downhill across the next field to climb another stile, bear left and continue downhill, passing between two ruined buildings and on down a most attractive tree-lined path to climb a stile onto a road (**E**).

Cross over the road, take the downhill tarmac track opposite, which is signposted 'Tabernacle Chapel', turn right to cross the stream and continue, passing to the right of the chapel. Shortly afterwards the track bends to the left and climbs gently along the eastern side of the valley. Go through a metal gate, keep ahead, pass to the right of a farm and continue, going through several more metal gates, up to the next farm, Upper House.

Go through a metal gate into the farmyard, turn right (**F**), in the direction of a yellow waymark, between the farmhouse and a barn, then turn left and continue up, going through another metal gate. Walk along an uphill track, passing through a metal gate onto open moorland, and bear slightly right to keep alongside a wall on the right. Where the wall turns to the right keep ahead along an obvious grassy track towards the ridge in front.

On meeting a broader track just before a group of conifers bear left onto it to continue along the side of the valley – this is a superb high-level walk with grand views. About 50 yards (46 m) after a fence on the right ends there is a fork; take the left-hand, narrower path which eventually descends into the valley of Cwm Nant Brân, meeting a wall on the left and keeping alongside it downhill. Turn left over a small stream, go through a gate and continue along a wooded path gently uphill to a farm. Turn left to pass between gateposts and, ignoring a waymark to the right, follow the track ahead which descends between thick conifers to the starting point.

Partrishow church

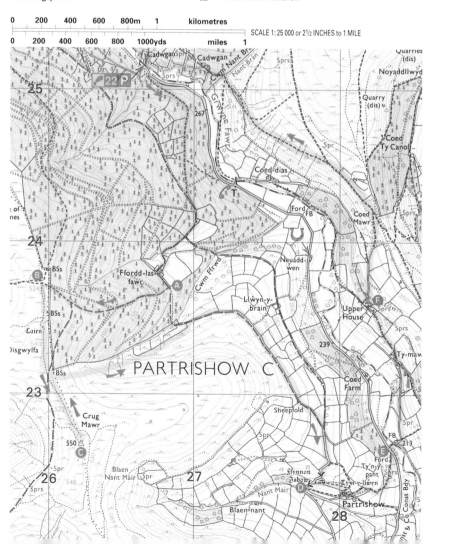

23 Two castles walk

Start:	Caerphilly. Shorter version starts from Caerphilly Common
Distance:	9½ miles (15.25 km). Shorter version 7½ miles (12 km)
Approximate time:	5 hours (4 hours for shorter version)
Parking:	Caerphilly. For shorter version use car park at top of Caerphilly Common
Refreshments:	Pubs and cafés at Caerphilly, pub just below Caerphilly Common
Ordnance Survey maps:	Landranger 171 (Cardiff, Newport and surrounding area), Pathfinder 1148, ST 08/18 (Pontypridd (South) & Caerphilly)

General description The two castles on this walk are Caerphilly and Castell Coch, very different in age, size, situation and function but in their varied ways two of the most interesting and impressive castles in Wales. The countryside between them comprises a mixture of open, bracken-covered common, grassy hilltop ridges and attractive woodland, and part of the route is along the eastern side of the Taff gorge. Although the noise of traffic can be heard in places, the unspoilt landscape and sense of peace and remoteness on much of the walk makes it difficult to believe that the route lies between the M4 and suburbs of Cardiff to the south and the former mining valleys to the north. This is quite a strenuous walk with several fairly stiff climbs. The shorter version, avoiding the long ascent and descent along the A469 from the centre of Caerphilly, starts from the car park at the top of Caerphilly Common a few yards south of point (**A**).

Powerful walls, towers, gatehouses and concentric fortifications, augmented by elaborate water defences, make Caerphilly the most strongly defended castle in Britain. Second only to Windsor in area, it even surpasses the great Edwardian castles of North Wales. Such complex and advanced defences were considered necessary because of the site; the castle lies in a shallow valley with no natural defences. It was built in the 1260s and 1270s by the powerful Gilbert de Clare, Earl of Gloucester, to protect his newly acquired territories in Glamorgan from the growing power of Llywelyn ap Gruffydd, last native Prince of Wales. In the end this formidable fortress saw little military action and faded into the usual obsolescence and decay, but many would justifiably claim that Caerphilly is not only the most impressive medieval castle in Britain but one of the great castles of Europe.

For the full walk, start by the castle entrance and war memorial and walk uphill away from the castle, turning first right and then left, crossing a railway bridge and continuing more steeply uphill onto the open expanses of Caerphilly Common. Near the top at a left-hand bend turn right off the road onto a path (**A**).

*The shorter version begins at a car park opposite the junction of the A469 and a minor road. Walk north along the A469 for a few yards and where the road bends right turn left onto a path (**A**).*

Follow the path uphill through bracken, bearing right and ignoring all side paths

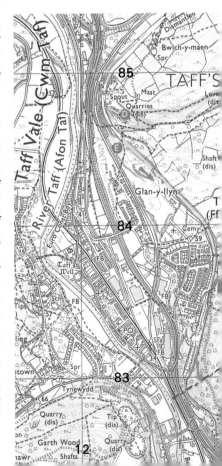

to head up to the highest point on the common (891 feet (271 m)), marked by a triangulation pillar. From here there is a magnificent all-round view that includes Cardiff and the Bristol Channel to the south, a line of ridges and rolling hills leading to the Taff valley to the west, Caerphilly town with its huge lake-girt castle below and beyond it the valleys and edge of the Brecon Beacons on the horizon to the north, and wooded hills to the east.

At the triangulation pillar bear slightly left along a narrow but clear downhill path, passing to the right of a wire fence surrounding a small reservoir and making for a road junction on the corner of the common. At a junction of paths near the bottom bear right to join the road at a Ffordd y Bryniau (Ridgeway Walk) footpath sign (**B**); these signs are followed on the next stage of the walk. Cross the road, take the path opposite and almost immediately turn right, at a meeting of paths, to continue across open, bracken-covered common. Take the left-hand path at the first fork and at the next fork ignore a yellow waymark to the right and turn left to follow a path downhill to a lane.

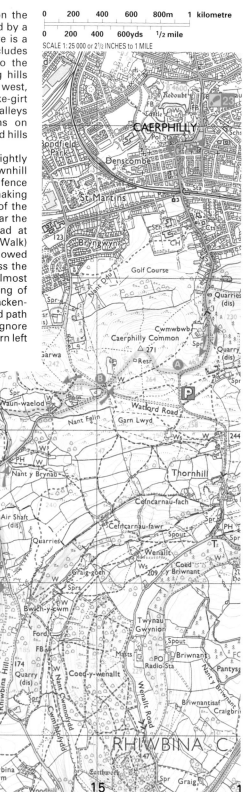

Caerphilly Castle

Do not go onto the lane but turn right along a track in front of a cottage, then turn left through a metal gate, bear slightly right and head across the middle of a field to another metal gate. Ahead is a fine view of Craig yr Allt. Go through the gate, continue across the next field, descending to a waymarked tree, and beyond that ford a stream and climb a stile onto a lane. Turn right and by the Rockwood Riding Centre turn sharp left (**C**) onto a narrower lane and follow it uphill for ¼ mile (0.5 km). Shortly after the lane levels off, pass through a metal gate and immediately bear right to go through another one.

Take the path that heads up along the flanks of Craig yr Allt, below the ridge on the right. Go through a metal gate and continue across another lovely, open, bracken-covered area interspersed with trees from where there are fine views over unspoilt, green, quiet countryside. It is difficult to believe that you are so close to Cardiff and the M4 just over the hills to the south and the former mining valleys a few miles to the north. At a fork take the right-hand, upper path, continuing steadily uphill across Craig yr Allt. There are views of Taff's Well below and the next prominent ridge of Garth Hill in front.

At the next fork keep along the left-hand, lower path. To the left is the Taff gorge through which river, railway and main road squeeze to reach the Welsh capital. The path starts to descend and at a T-junction of paths leave the Ridgeway Walk by turning left (**D**), following the direction of a 'Circular Walk' footpath sign, along a path that bends sharply left and heads downhill to a gate. Go through, turn right and walk across a small, open grassy area before continuing along an obvious path that bears left towards trees.

On entering the trees turn sharply to the right at a junction of paths, head down, climb a stile and continue downhill to go through a metal gate. Keep ahead over a disused railway bridge, follow the path as it curves left downhill, turn left to a metal gate, pass through a gap beside it, and turn right onto a disused railway track to join the Taff Trail (**E**).

Follow this pleasant, tree-lined track for ¾ mile (1.25 km) before heading up to a junction of paths and tracks on the edge of the woodland of Fforest-fawr. Turn left here, following Taff Trail signs, along a track which soon bends right and continues steadily uphill through this delightful woodland above the Taff gorge. Later the track levels off and reaches a T-junction (**F**). Here turn right, pass through a wooden barrier and follow a winding track downhill to the parking area in front of Castell Coch (**G**).

Castell Coch looks like a fantasy castle, and in many ways it is. This Victorian structure was built for the Marquess of Bute, on the site of a ruined medieval castle, to fulfil a rich man's desire to create an authentic reconstruction of a thirteenth-century Welsh castle, even complete with drawbridge and portcullis. The interior is lavishly decorated and the castle's fairytale appearance is further enhanced by its romantic location perched above the thickly wooded Taff gorge.

Turn left along the drive down to the entrance to the castle grounds and just before reaching a road turn left onto an uphill path signposted to Taff Gorge Countryside Centre. Pass beside a metal barrier – the countryside centre is just to the right – and continue ahead steadily uphill through woodland, keeping along the main path all the while. Shortly after a sharp left-hand bend the path bends right to reach a crossroads of tracks and paths (**H**). Turn right along a broad track and follow it through Fforest-fawr for ¾ mile (1.25 km), eventually passing beside a metal barrier and continuing through a car park to reach a lane on the edge of the woodland (**J**).

Bear left uphill, bear left again on joining a road and continue steadily uphill for nearly ½ mile (0.75 km) to a fork. Here take the right-hand road, passing the Black Cock Inn, and continue uphill for another ½ mile (0.75 km) to emerge onto Caerphilly Common. At a T-junction cross the road and keep ahead onto the common. After a few yards bear right to pick up the outward route and retrace your steps over the highest point on the common to return to the start. □

24 Waterfalls walk

Start:	Porth yr Ogof. On minor road 1 mile (1.5 km) south of Ystradfellte
Distance:	9½ miles (15.25 km)
Approximate time:	6 hours
Parking:	Car park at Porth yr Ogof
Refreshments:	Pubs at Pontneddfechan
Ordnance Survey maps:	Landranger 160 (Brecon Beacons), Outdoor Leisure 11 (Brecon Beacons – Central area)

General description *There can be few more exhilarating and satisfying walks than this. On the southern edge of Fforest Fawr, where the sandstone that underlies most of the Brecon Beacons National Park gives way to a band of limestone, the rivers Mellte, Hepste, Pyrddin and Neath flow through wooded ravines and plunge over a series of waterfalls, the highest concentration of falls in Wales. All of them are spectacular but probably the most exciting part of the walk comes when the path passes behind the great sheet of water at Sgwd yr Eira. The walk is lengthy and quite energetic, mostly through or above the thickly wooded gorges, with plenty of ascents and descents and some fairly difficult sections over rocky terrain and muddy paths. Simply take your time and watch your step, for this is a walk to be enjoyed to the full and well worth taking slowly.*

Refer to map overleaf.

The huge cave entrance of Porth yr Ogof is just below the car park and is reached by steps. Here the River Mellte is swallowed up and disappears underground to emerge about ¼ mile (0.5 km) to the south. Leave the car park, cross the road and take the path straight ahead, at a public footpath sign to 'Blue Pool and Clun-gwyn Waterfalls'. After a few yards turn first left in front of a wire fence and then right over a triple stile to continue along a very rocky path. Make your way over boulders and pass between potholes to emerge onto a grassy area beside the River Mellte which has now reappeared. Continue along an undulating path by the river, going through two gates and passing a footbridge. There are a number of 'Danger' signs warning of very steep, rough, slippery ground and at the second of these signs turn left uphill, by a fence on the right, and bear right onto a higher path to continue along the right-hand edge of conifer woodland.

Shortly afterwards descend between fences to the first of the series of falls, Sgŵd Clun-gwyn (**A**). From here continue above the river, but at the next 'Danger' sign turn left and head uphill along a curving path through woodland. Bear right to continue high up above the river, once more along the right-hand edge of conifers, passing above the falls of Sgŵd Isaf Clun-gwyn and Sgŵd y Pannwr which can be glimpsed through the trees. Later the path curves left away from the River Mellte to continue above the gorge of the River Hepste and soon the impressive fall of Sgwd yr Eira can be seen ahead. Soon after sighting the fall turn right, at a public footpath sign, down a steep flight of steps which twist and turn sharply, and follow the steps down to the bottom of the gorge.

Continue along to Sgwd yr Eira – take care as the path is difficult in places. Now comes the most exciting part of the walk and an unusual experience as you turn right to pass behind the fall (**B**). Be careful as the rocks are slippery, although you should not get wet. On the other side climb quite steeply along a rocky, curving path, turning sharp right at a yellow waymark to continue twisting and turning up steps. At the top turn right at a public footpath sign, following directions for Pontneddfechan and Craig y Ddinas, and continue along the top of the gorge. Soon the path bears left away from the river to continue through a mixture of woodland and more open moorland; keep following the regular waymarks and footpath signs to Craig y Ddinas (Dinas Rock). At a public footpath sign for Dinas Rock car park bear right along the broad ridge of Craig y

Sgwd Gwladus – the Lady Waterfall

Ddinas, noted for its former silica mine workings, above two rivers. Soon the path heads downhill to the car park. Turn right to cross the bridge over the River Mellte and then left (**C**) along a road beside the river into Pontneddfechan.

Walk through the village and in front of the Angel pub turn right (**D**), go through a metal gate inscribed 'Sgwd Gwladus – Lady Waterfall' and continue along a broad, level track, the bed of a disused tramway. This is a delightful section – one of the easiest of the walk – keeping beside the rushing waters of the River Neath (Nedd Fechan). Climb a stile and shortly afterwards the track narrows to a path; follow it as far as a footbridge just beyond the confluence of the Neath and Pyrddin (**E**). Turn right over the bridge to a footpath sign on the other side and turn left for a short detour to view Sgwd Gwladus, which some would consider the most beautiful of all the falls in its lovely, wooded amphitheatre.

Retrace your steps to the footbridge and keep ahead to another one a few yards ahead. Do not cross it but continue above the left bank of the River Neath, following the footpath sign to Pont Melin-fach. This is another lovely section of the walk, passing several small falls and with fine views up the river. Turn right over a footbridge and continue by the river, passing Scwd Ddwli, eventually climbing a stile and bearing left through a car park to a bridge (Pont Melin-fach) (**F**). Turn right to cross the bridge and turn left over a stile at a public footpath sign to Pont Rhyd-y-canu. Although the sign indicates that you keep ahead by the river, it is better to turn right and climb to a higher path in order to avoid an awkward rocky section – the two paths soon meet. Now follow an undulating path along the right bank of the River Neath, climbing two stiles, to the next bridge (Pont Rhyd-y-cnau) (**G**).

At the bridge turn right, at a public footpath sign to Gwaun Bryn-bwch, along a track that winds steadily uphill through woodland. On emerging from the trees continue uphill and go through a metal gate onto a lane. Turn right along the lane, which bends right to a T-junction. Turn left and after a few yards bear right (**H**) through a metal gate, at a public bridleway sign to Porth yr Ogof, along a track that heads gently downhill. At a blue-waymarked post turn left off the track, go through a metal gate and continue gently downhill along an enclosed path, passing through a series of gates to reach the road opposite the car park at the start. □

25 Waun Fach

Start:	Castell Dinas. Small parking area up unsigned lane ¹/₄ mile (0.5 km) north of Castle Inn at Pengenffordd
Distance:	7 miles (11.25 km)
Approximate time:	4¹/₂ hours
Parking:	Parking area at Castell Dinas
Refreshments:	Pub at Pengenffordd
Ordnance Survey maps:	Landranger 161 (Abergavenny & The Black Mountains), Outdoor Leisure 13 (Brecon Beacons – Eastern area)

General description *After an optional short, steep climb at the start of the walk to the scanty remains of Castell Dinas, a magnificent viewpoint, the rest of the route to the 2,660-foot (810 m) summit of Waun Fach, the highest point in the Black Mountains, is a lengthy and steady rather than strenuous ascent. The latter part of the walk involves an exhilarating ramble along a switchback ridge. Route finding could be difficult and potentially hazardous in bad weather, especially misty conditions, therefore save this walk for a fine day when the extensive views can be enjoyed to the full.*

There are two alternative routes from the start to point (**B**) – one fairly strenuous but infinitely more scenic, the other easy.

For the more strenuous route start by walking along the enclosed track that begins at a public footpath sign where the narrow tarmac lane ends at the parking area. Pass to the right of a farm, bear right uphill and at a fork bear right again and go through a metal gate. Keep ahead over the brow and turn right (**A**) over a stile to climb steeply to the earthworks and fragmentary remains of Castell Dinas. This excellent defensive site has been used both as an Iron Age hill fort and as a Norman castle and at 1,476 feet (450 m) must be one of the highest castles in the country. Continue over the top, which is a magnificent viewpoint, keep ahead towards a fence and turn right to head downhill, bearing right to follow the curve of the castle mound to a waymarked post. Turn left here in the direction of a white arrow – this is a permissive path – and head quite steeply downhill across the

field to climb a stile. Continue downhill by a wire fence on the right, pass through an area of gorse and climb another stile at the bottom of the field. Continue downhill, still by a wire fence on the right, cross a narrow stream in the valley bottom, climb a stile immediately ahead and bear slightly right to continue alongside a wire fence bordering woodland on the right. Climb another stile onto a track and turn left along it (**B**).

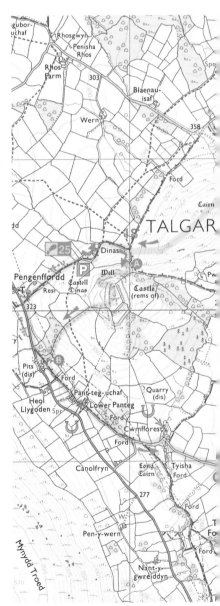

For the easier alternative for this first part of the walk, from the parking area walk back along the lane to the main road and turn left along a hedge-lined track parallel to it, passing a stile at (**B**).

Keep along this enclosed, hedge- and tree-lined track, passing behind the Castle Inn. Bear left at a fork, later ford a stream and keep ahead to a lane at a U-bend. Bear slightly left along the lane, which heads downhill, then turns right in front of Cwmfforest Riding Stables and continues uphill to a T-junction. Turn right and shortly turn left (**C**) onto an enclosed track, following it steadily uphill and passing through several gates to eventually emerge onto open moorland.

There is now a long, steady, continuous climb along a clearly defined path from which there are superb views to the right down the valley towards the round keep

SCALE 1:25 000 or 2½ INCHES to 1 MILE

Looking towards Pen y Manllwyn from the summit of Waun Fach

of Tretower Castle in the distance. The path veers slightly right to continue to the cairn which can just be seen on the ridge ahead. On arriving at this cairn (**D**) you are rewarded with a magnificent all-round view: to the right the long ridge leading to Pen Cerrig-calch, ahead the cairn on Pen y Gadair Fawr, to the left the long ridge that curves right to the dome of Waun Fach, and behind Mynydd Troed and the line of the Brecon Beacons.

At the cairn turn left onto the grassy path that runs along the top of the ridge – not onto the wider, parallel track that runs below it. The path heads quite steeply uphill onto the crest of the ridge and continues along it, following it as it curves right around the head of the valley, heading gently up to the bare, rounded summit of Waun Fach (**E**). This part of the walk is likely to be muddy as the surface is peaty and badly drained; the summit is marked by a concrete plinth surrounded by a morass of peat. For the highest point on the Black Mountains it is a rather undistinguished summit, but nevertheless another magnificent viewpoint.

From the summit turn left onto a downhill path that can be seen heading across the next ridge, Pen y Manllwyn. From here there is a superb view ahead of Y Grib, a connecting spur to the main

ridge which curves left in a roller-coaster fashion; the route later uses this to return to the start.

Soon after passing the cairn on Pen y Manllwyn turn left (**F**) off the path to descend steeply to the lower connecting ridge. There is no precise landmark at which to do this and no obvious path but it is easy to descend the smooth grass and heather flanks of the ridge. Look out for and make for a cairn and here pick up a reasonably distinct path which continues downhill, later flattening out for a while as it keeps along the ever-narrowing ridge.

Now comes an exhilarating finale on a switchback route along the crest of the long, narrow ridge of Y Grib, with some fairly steep climbs and descents. All the way there are grand views on both sides, and ahead to Mynydd Troed, the Usk valley and the main Brecon Beacons range. If you wish to avoid some of the steep 'ups and downs' there are some easier alternative paths that contour along the sides. On the final descent Castell Dinas, with its concentric earthworks, is directly in front.

On this last descent bear right, head steeply downhill towards a wire fence and climb a stile a few yards to the right of a metal gate in the field corner. Keep ahead to join a track and follow it back to the start. □

26 Fan y Big and Taf Fechan Forest

Start:	Torpantau
Distance:	8 miles (12.75 km)
Approximate time:	4½ hours
Parking:	Forestry Commission's Talybont car park at Torpantau
Refreshments:	None
Ordnance Survey maps:	Landranger 160 (Brecon Beacons), Outdoor Leisure 11 (Brecon Beacons – Central area)

General description After an initial steep climb, the rest of this walk in the heart of the Brecon Beacons is relatively relaxing. The climb is to the ridges of Craig y Fan Ddu and later Graig Fan Las which the walk follows to reach the main north-facing escarpment of the Beacons. After a dramatic stretch along the curving rim of the escarpment to the summit of Fan y Big, the route descends to the 'Gap Road' and follows this trackway, which is thought to be Roman, above the Neuadd reservoirs. Finally there is a pleasant, scenic stroll along the Taff Trail through the woodlands of Taf Fechan Forest.

On the escarpment of the Brecon Beacons

Although a comparatively easy mountain walk, much of it is along the edge of steep escarpments and therefore do not attempt it in winter or in misty weather unless properly experienced and equipped for such conditions.

Refer to map overleaf.

Begin by walking back to the car park entrance and immediately turn right onto an uphill path, by a wire fence on the right and above a steam and waterfalls on the left. Follow the wire fence as it curves round to the right and after it ends keep straight ahead, more steeply uphill, to reach a cairn at the top of the ridge. To the right there are superb views over the Talybont valley to the long ridges of the Black Mountains on the horizon.

Continue along the peaty, badly drained ridge top of Craig y Fan Ddu and ahead is the impressive, sweeping, smooth curve of the ridge of Graig Fan Las. Later bear right to ford a stream and continue, curving gradually right along Graig Fan Las and enjoying the magnificent open, empty views to the right over mountain and forest. When you eventually reach the main escarpment of the Brecon Beacons turn sharp left (**A**).

Keep along the clear, well-used path to the summit of Fan y Big, following the edge of the escarpment as it bends left and later curves right around the head of the valley of Cwm Oergwm. This is a typical Beacons landscape of sweeping, bare, smooth curves, steep escarpments, flat summits and wide vistas, with views beyond of the gentler scenery of the Usk valley and the houses of Brecon. On reaching Fan y Big's rather unremarkable summit (**B**) turn sharp left, still walking along the edge of the escarpment, to descend into the broad col of Bwlch ar y Fan which lies between Fan y Big and Cribyn. Ahead looms the abrupt and daunting-looking peak of Cribyn, to the left the Upper Neuadd reservoir can be seen and to the right there is a view down Cwm Cynwyn to the Usk valley.

At the col turn left (**C**) along a broad, flat, stony track, which is thought to be of Roman origin and is usually referred to as the 'Gap Road' because it makes use of the gap in the escarpment. Follow this trackway above the Upper Neuadd reservoir and after 1½ miles (2.5 km), where the main track turns right (**D**), there is a choice of routes. If the stream below is fordable, bear left and head steeply down a rocky track to ford it, head up the other side and continue along the right-hand edge of conifers to descend gently to a road. Otherwise, follow the main track to

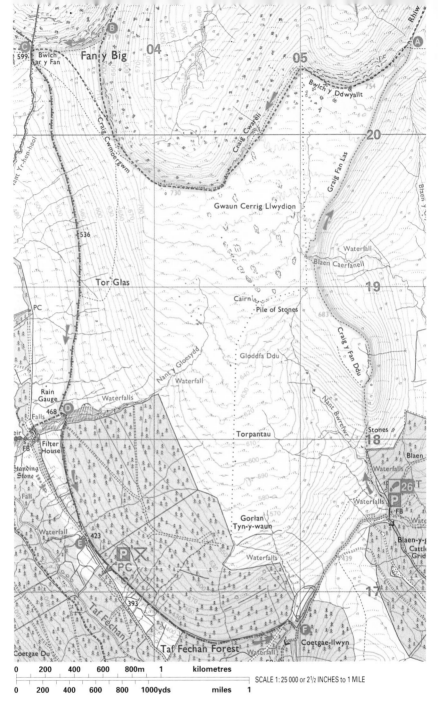

the right down to a metal gate, turn left onto a path in front of it, cross the stream, climb a stile and continue along the road ahead. The track and road meet at a Taff Trail footpath sign (**E**).

Here keep straight ahead along a flat, grassy track which is part of the Taff Trail. It runs to the left of the road, by a wire fence on the right and along the edge

of the conifers of Taf Fechan Forest. Ahead are most attractive views towards Talybont reservoir. The track passes through several gates and continues through woodland, eventually bending right to cross a stream and rejoin the road (**F**). Turn left and follow the road uphill for just over ½ mile (0.75 km) to return to the start. □

27 Craig-y-nos, Cribarth and the Henrhyd Falls

Start:	Craig-y-nos Country Park
Distance:	8½ miles (13.5 km)
Approximate time:	4½ hours
Parking:	Craig-y-nos Country Park
Refreshments:	Tearooms at Craig-y-nos, pub at Abercrave, café at Henrhyd Falls
Ordnance Survey maps:	Landranger 160 (Brecon Beacons), Outdoor Leisure 12 (Brecon Beacons – Western area)

General description *Craig-y-nos Country Park, formerly the grounds of a large house, is the starting point for this lengthy and unusually varied walk in Glyn Tawe, the upper reaches of the Swansea valley on the southern fringes of the Black Mountain. The walk includes open hillside, a summit, woodland, riverside, a narrow ravine and the highest waterfall in South Wales, as well as having the historic interest of Craig-y-nos and the former quarrying activities in the area. In addition to being lengthy, this is a quite energetic walk with several ascents and descents but well worth while for the superb views and scenic contrasts.*

Refer to map overleaf.

In 1878 the tempestuous, internationally famous opera singer Adelina Patti fell in love with the romantic setting of Craig-y-nos Castle in the upper Swansea valley

The Henrhyd Falls

and the following year she bought it. Over the next twelve years she enlarged and modernised the early-nineteenth-century castle and laid out over forty acres of ornamental grounds. Such was her fame and wealth that at the nearby station she had her own railway carriage and a private waiting room for herself and her many distinguished visitors, who included the Prince of Wales, later Edward VII. After her death in 1919 the castle became a hospital and it is now a restaurant and function centre. In 1976 the grounds – woodland, meadow, lakes and river – were acquired by the Brecon Beacons National Park and after many years of neglect they have been restored as a country park.

Turn left out of the car park, follow the main road for about 200 yards (183 m), passing in front of the nineteenth-century castle buildings, and at a public footpath sign turn right over a stile (**A**). Keep to the right of a farm, climbing a series of stiles, and at the end of the farm buildings bear right in the direction of a public footpath sign along an uphill path to begin the ascent of Cribarth.

Follow this clear path steeply uphill, curving slightly left all the while and later continuing in a straight line along a less steep, grassy path to a gate. Go through, bear left and continue gently uphill to enter a kind of natural amphitheatre encircled by hills. Pass through a hollow in the hills and continue below the ridge on the right, joining and keeping by a wall and later a wire fence on the left. The triangulation pillar on the summit of Cribarth (1,390 feet (423 m)) can be seen ahead; bear right and head up to it (**B**) for the magnificent all-round view that takes in the hilly moorlands of Fforest Fawr, almost the whole length of the Swansea valley, the hills that guard the northern end of the former mining valleys and the barren, empty wilderness of the Black Mountain.

From the summit descend quite steeply to rejoin and keep along the main path below, again by a wall on the left, heading downhill. At a wall corner a disused quarry tramroad can be seen contouring along the side of the hill ahead but at this point you turn left and make your way between boulders to a stile and footpath sign about 50 yards (46 m) ahead. Climb the stile and, following the direction of a yellow waymark to the right, continue along a grassy path that contours around the slopes of Cribarth, keeping parallel to a wall and a wire fence on the right.

The path gradually bears left following the curve of the hill and heads down to a short marker-post, and beyond that to a stile. Do not climb the stile but turn left, in the direction of a public footpath sign to Ynyswen, and continue through rocks, bracken and heather along the southern flanks of Cribarth. Go through a metal gate, keep ahead – now by a wire fence on the right – go through a second gate and continue down to a third one at the top edge of woodland. Go through the gate to a fork (C) and take the right-hand track to descend through the beautiful, steep-sided Abercrave Wood to a metal gate in front of a barn.

Go through, keep ahead, pass through the right-hand one of two metal gates opposite and continue along a track by a stream on the right. Keeping to the right of farm buildings go through a metal gate and turn right along a tarmac drive. At a junction by the Abercrave Inn turn sharp left (D) down a road and take the first turning on the right along a road that first bends sharply to the right and then turns left to cross a bridge over the River Tawe.

On the other side of the bridge turn left at a public footpath sign, go through a kissing-gate to the left of a house and continue along a tarmac path beside the river. Go through a second kissing-gate, pass under a road, go through a third one and keep ahead to a footpath sign. Turn left to keep alongside the river, below sloping woodland, and a few yards further on follow the direction of a waymarked post to bear slightly right uphill and continue through woodland above the river. Head up to keep by a

0   200   400   600   800m   1 kilometre

0   200   400   600yds   ½ mile

SCALE 1: 25 000 or 2½ INCHES to 1 MILE

hedge-bank and line of trees on the right, climb a stile, continue along the left-hand edge of a field, above the top edge of the woodland and by a wire fence on the left, and climb another stile onto a lane (**E**).

Turn left along the lane for nearly ½ mile (0.75 km), keep left at a fork, descend steeply and follow the lane around a right-hand bend to Llech Bridge. Cross the bridge, continue along the lane for about 50 yards (46 m) and at a public footpath sign turn right over a stile (**F**). There is now a most attractive part of the walk along an undulating path by the side of the beautiful gorge of the River Llech to the Henrhyd Falls. The path is mostly high up above the river, with steps in places and several stiles and footbridges. Approaching the falls the route continues by bearing left along an uphill path, but for a better view keep ahead, turn right over a footbridge and turn left to continue to the impressive falls which at just under 100 feet (30 m) are the highest in South Wales. They are now owned by the National Trust. Retrace your steps to take the steep uphill path, go through two gates at the top and continue through a car park to a road (**G**).

Turn left along the road (if you wish to visit the café turn right over the bridge) and at a left-hand bend by a mast (**H**) climb a stile and keep ahead – there is no obvious path – across an area of rough and boggy pasture, bearing slightly left and heading down to cross a footbridge. Continue in the same direction to a stile, climb it and head gently uphill towards the right-hand edge of the line of trees in front. Here bear right alongside a fence on the left, go through a gap in a wire fence ahead and, keeping by a hedge-bank and fence on the left, bear left and head downhill by a stream on the right.

Climb a stile onto a lane (**J**), turn right over a bridge and follow the lane for ½ mile (0.75 km), heading downhill. There are superb views both of Cribarth and along the Tawe valley to the prominent Carmarthen Fans on the skyline. Where the lane turns left to cross Pen-y-cae Bridge keep ahead (**K**), at a public bridleway sign, along a tarmac drive. In front of a metal gate continue along an enclosed, tree-lined path, bearing left to cross a footbridge over a stream and continuing to a lane. Keep ahead along the lane, which later joins a wider one.

Just after passing a bungalow on the right, bear left (**L**) along a tarmac, hedge-lined track. Where this ends in front of a farm bear left again through a metal gate, passing to the left of the farmhouse, and continue along an enclosed path. Later the path keeps along the right-hand edge of woodland, by a wire fence on the left and below steep rocky slopes on the right. At a fork take the left-hand, downhill path towards some stepping-stones. Go through a gate but do not cross the river. Instead turn left (**M**) over a stile to re-enter Craig-y-nos Country Park and walk beside the River Tawe, between trees and through a picnic area. Turn right to cross a footbridge over the river and go through the gate ahead to return to the start. □

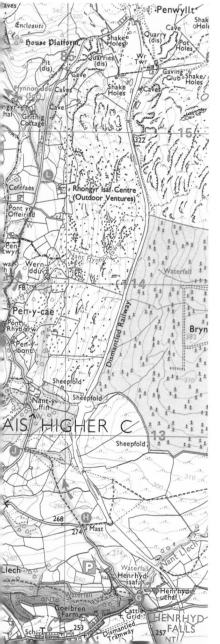

28 Brecon Beacons horseshoe

Start:	Cwm Gwdi. From Brecon cross bridge over River Usk, turn left opposite Drovers Arms along Ffrwdgrech Road, follow signs to Cwm Gwdi Training Camp, go through camp entrance and car park is at far end
Distance:	9½ miles (15.25 km)
Approximate time:	6 hours
Parking:	Car park at Cwm Gwdi Training Camp
Refreshments:	None
Ordnance Survey maps:	Landranger 160 (Brecon Beacons), Outdoor Leisure 11 (Brecon Beacons – Central area)

General description *This walk, which includes the three main peaks of the Brecon Beacons, is arguably the finest mountain walk in South Wales and one of the best in the country. A lengthy, gradual, steadily ascending approach leads to the foot of Cribyn, then the final climb up to its summit (2,608 feet (795 m)) is steep and exhausting. A descent into a col is followed by another steep, though short, pull up to Pen y Fan (2,907 feet (886 m)), the highest point in the Brecon Beacons and the highest point in Britain south of Snowdonia. A much gentler descent and ascent leads onto the distinctive flat summit of Corn Du (2,863 feet (873 m)). The return route drops down to the beautiful little lake of Llyn Cwm Llwch, and this is followed by a relaxing stroll through the lovely valley of Cwm Llwch. This is a walk worth taking plenty of time over; the approach and return are every bit as enjoyable as the three peaks themselves and the views are magnificent. But do not attempt it in poor, especially misty, weather, unless experienced in such conditions and able to use a compass.*

Refer to map overleaf.

Begin by heading down to a stile in the fence below the car park. Climb it, cross a footbridge over a stream (Nant Gwdi), bear left up steps and continue along a rather indistinct path through woodland, initially keeping parallel with the stream below on the left. Later bear right to pick up and keep by a wire fence on the left – the path now becomes clearer – heading across open grassland to a footpath sign by a gate (the sign points back to Cwm Gwdi car park) (**A**).

Turn left through the gate and follow an enclosed track – it might be easier to walk along the edge of the field to the right because of mud and overhanging branches – down to a stile, climb it and keep ahead to a T-junction (**B**). Turn right along a track, follow the waymarks through a farmyard and climb a stile at the end of the farm buildings. Bear right slightly uphill, in the direction of the yellow, not the blue, waymark, making for the top right-hand corner of a field. Pass through a gap in a line of trees, continue along the right-hand edge of the field, by a line of trees and a wire fence on the right, climb a stile and keep ahead downhill across the next field to climb another one. Continue in the same direction across the next field, climb a stile at the far end, turn left along an enclosed track and climb another stile onto a tarmac track.

Pen y Fan – the highest point in southern Britain

Turn right along it, first heading downhill to cross a stream and then continuing uphill. This is the start of a steady, unremitting climb of 2¼ miles (3.5 km) to the summit of Cribyn. Where the tarmac track ends keep ahead along an enclosed stony track and go through a gate onto the open mountain-side by a National Trust sign for Cwm Cynwyn.

At first keep by a wall on the left but shortly bear right off the main track to follow the distinct grassy path that can be seen heading uphill in front. To the left is a fine view across Cwm Cynwyn to Fan y Big and later, at the brow of the hill, there is a superb view of the main ridge of the Brecon Beacons with Fan y Big to the left, the abrupt north face of Cribyn straight ahead and the distinctive bulk of Pen y Fan to the right. Now there is a flattish stretch before the final, steep, daunting-looking, head-on assault on the summit of Cribyn (**C**). The reward is a magnificent view which includes Fan y Big, the Black Mountains, Llangorse Lake, Brecon, the Usk valley, the hills of mid Wales, Pen y Fan, Corn Du and the peaks and reservoirs to the south.

Turn right and make for the summit of Pen y Fan along a clear, broad, badly eroded path, heading steeply down into a col and equally steeply uphill again, with a final, rocky scramble to the cairn that marks the summit (**D**). From here there is an even more spectacular view because it includes Fforest Fawr and the Black Mountain to the west and the beautiful little lake of Llyn Cwm Llwch below. Now bear left and make your way to the third of the trio of summits, the flat-topped Corn Du – thankfully there is only a modest descent and ascent this time.

From the summit cairn on Corn Du (**E**) keep in the same direction and after an initial steep descent continue along the edge of the escarpment above Llyn Cwm Llwch. The memorial passed by is to Tommy Jones, a five-year-old boy whose body was found here in 1900. He was walking over the mountains and died after becoming separated from his companions and losing his way. Shortly after the monument follow the path that descends quite steeply towards the left-hand side of the lake. From this path there are spectacular views of the great natural

The abrupt north face of Cribyn

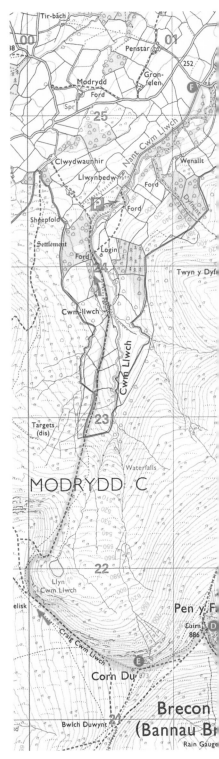

amphitheatre formed by Corn Du and Pen y Fan that encloses the lake, and of the lovely green valley of Cwm Llwch with Brecon and the gentler landscapes of the Usk valley beyond.

Keep above Llyn Cwm Llwch and bear slightly left to continue through the valley, keeping to the left of the stream all the way. This is an outstandingly attractive and relaxing section of the walk; the path is clear and easy to follow and there are constant superb views. At first you head fairly gently downhill across open grassland to climb a stile by a National Trust sign for Cwm Llwch. Then continue through the increasingly more gentle and wooded terrain and just in front of a cottage turn left over a waymarked stile. Turn right to climb another one, keep ahead by a wall on the right, and soon after the wall ends curve first to the right and then turn left to continue along a delightful, tree-lined track enclosed by low walls, with the stream close by.

Climb a stile, then cross a footbridge over a tributary stream and continue beside the stream to reach a parking area. Pass through it, go through a metal gate and continue along the track ahead, which soon becomes a tarmac track. At a crossroads turn right (**F**), cross the stream and follow a narrow lane for 1 mile (1.5 km), keeping ahead at a junction, to the entrance to Cwm Gwdi Training Camp. Turn right through the entrance to return to the start. □

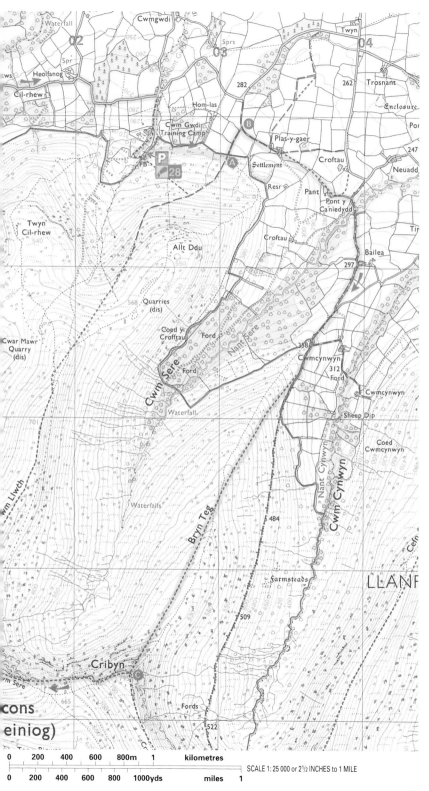

SCALE 1:25 000 or 2½ INCHES to 1 MILE

Useful organisations

The Countryside Commission
John Dower House, Crescent Place,
Cheltenham, Gloucestershire GL50 3RA.
Tel: 0242 521381

The Countryside Council for Wales
Plas Penrhos, Fford Penrhos, Bangor,
Gwynedd LL5 72LQ. Tel: 0248 370444

The National Trust
36 Queen Anne's Gate, London SW1H 9AS.
Tel: 071 222 9251
(South Wales Regional Office, The King's
Head, Bridge Street, Llandeilo, Dyfed
SA19 6BB. Tel: 0558 822800)

Council for National Parks
246 Lavender Hill, London SW11 1LJ.
Tel: 071 924 4077

Brecon Beacons National Park
7 Glamorgan Street, Brecon, Powys
LD3 7DP. Tel: 0874 624437

National park information centres can be
found at:
Abergavenny (Tel: 0873 853254)
Brecon (Tel: 0874 623156)
Craig-y-nos Country Park (Tel: 0639 730395)
Llandovery (Tel: 0550 20693)
Brecon Beacons Mountain Centre near
Libanus (Tel: 0874 623366)

Mid Glamorgan County Council
County Planning Department, Greyfriars
Road, Cardiff CF1 3LG. Tel: 0222 820820

Glamorgan Coast Heritage Centre
Dunraven Park, Southerndown, Mid
Glamorgan CF32 0RP. Tel: 0656 880157
or 880646

The Ramblers' Association
1/5 Wandsworth Road, London SW8 2XX.
Tel: 071 582 6878

The Forestry Commission
Information Branch, 231 Corstorphine Road,
Edinburgh EH12 7AT. Tel: 031 334 0303

The Youth Hostels Association
Trevelyan House, 8 St Stephen's Hill,
St Albans, Hertfordshire AL1 2DY.
Tel: 0727 855215

The Long Distance Walkers' Association
7 Ford Drive, Yarnfield, Stone, Staffordshire
ST15 0RP.

The Council for the Protection of Rural Wales
Ty Gwyn, 31 High Street, Welshpool, Powys
SY21 7JP. Tel: 0938 552525

Ordnance Survey
Romsey Road, Maybush, Southampton
SO9 4DH. Tel: 0703 792763/4/5 or 792792

Ordnance Survey maps of the Brecon Beacons and Glamorgan

The Brecon Beacons and Glamorgan are
covered by Ordnance Survey 1:50 000 scale
(1¼ inches to 1 mile, 2 cm to 1 km) Landranger
map sheets 160, 161, 170, 171 and 172. These
all-purpose maps are packed with information
to help you explore the area. Viewpoints, picnic
sites, places of interest, and caravan and
camping sites are shown, as well as public
rights of way information such as footpaths
and bridleways.

To examine the area in more detail, and
especially if you are planning walks, Ordnance
Survey Pathfinder maps at 1:25 000 scale
(2½ inches to 1 mile, 4 cm to 1 km) are ideal.
Maps covering this area are:

1036 (SN 63/73)	1084 (SN 81/91)
1037 (SN 83/93)	1086 (SO 21/31)
1038 (SO 03/13)	1107 (SN 60/70)
1060 (SN 62/72)	1108 (SO 80/90)
1083 (SN 61/71)	1110 (SO 20/30)

1111 (SO 40)	1148 (ST 08/18)
1127 (SS 69/79)	1149 (ST 28/38)
1128 (SS 89/99)	1150 (ST 48/58)
1129 (ST 09/19)	1163 (SS 87/96/97)
1130 (ST 29/39)	1164 (ST 07)
1131 (ST 49/59)	1165 (ST 17/27)
1146 (SS 78/88)	1180 (ST 06/16)
1147 (SS 98)	

Outdoor Leisure maps 11 (Brecon Beacons –
Central area), 12 (Brecon Beacons – Western
area) and 13 (Brecon Beacons – Eastern area)
cover parts of the Brecon Beacons and
Glamorgan and are also at 1:25 000 scale
(2½ inches to 1 mile, 4 cm to 1 km).

To get to the Brecon Beacons and
Glamorgan, use the Ordnance Survey
Travelmaster map number 1, Great Britain,
at 1:625 000 scale (1 inch to 10 miles, 1 cm to
6.25 km), or Travelmaster map number 7, Wales
and the West Midlands, or Travelmaster map
number 8, South West England and South
Wales, at 1:250 000 scale (1 inch to 4 miles,
1 cm to 2.5 km).

Ordnance Survey maps and guides are
available from most booksellers, stationers and
newsagents.

Index